The Art of One-Line Drawing

ATTABEIRA GERMAN DE TUROWSKI

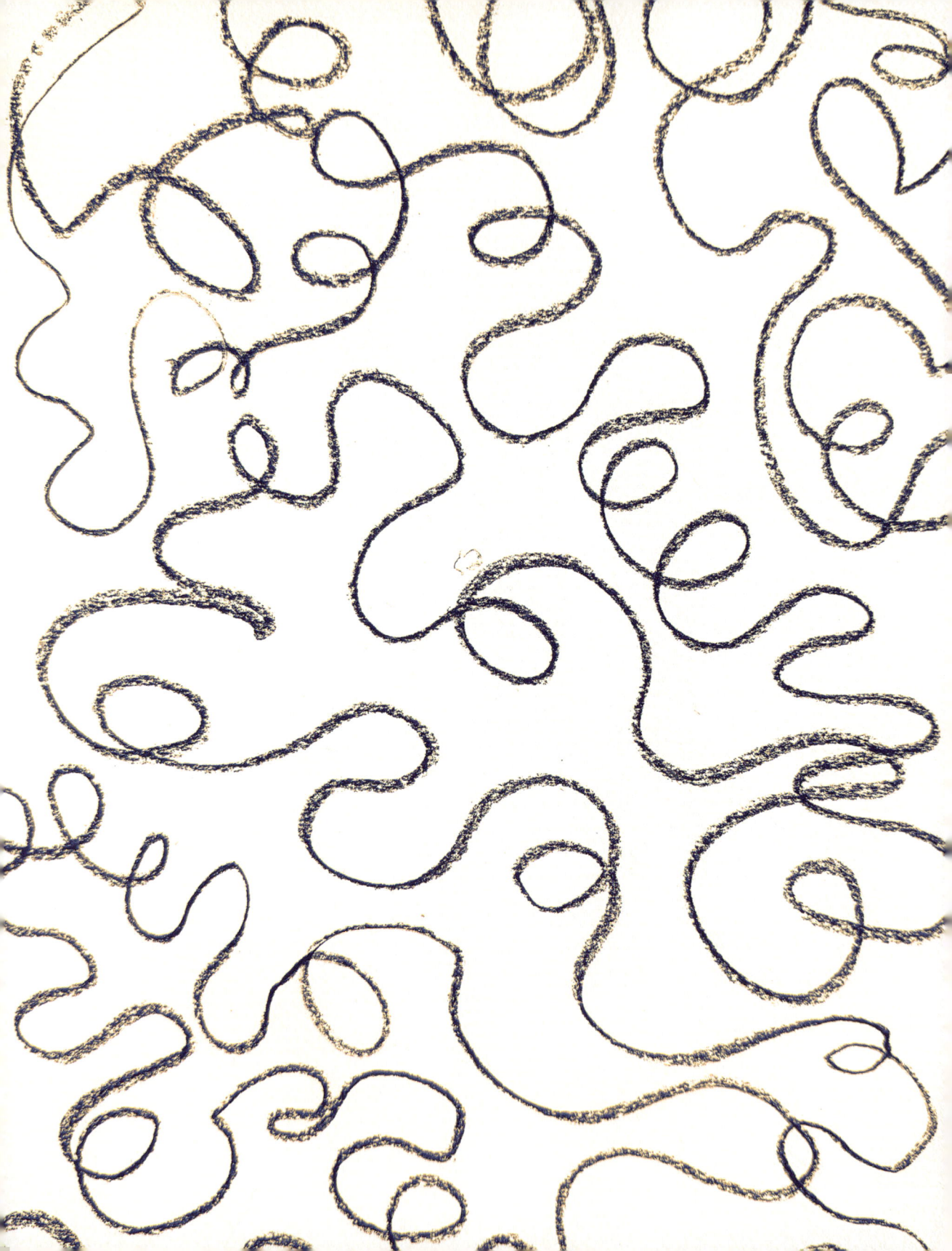

the art of
ONE-LINE DRAWING

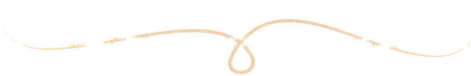

A Step-by-Step Guide to Creating
Beautiful Continuous Line Drawings

ATTABEIRA GERMAN DE TUROWSKI

rockynook

The Art of One-Line Drawing
A Step-by-Step Guide to Creating Beautiful
Continuous Line Drawings
Attabeira German de Turowski

Editor: Kelly Reed
Project manager: Lisa Brazieal
Marketing coordinator: Katie Walker
Copyeditor: Patricia Pane
Cover design: John Calmeyer
Interior design: John Calmeyer
Cover Illustration: Attabeira German de Turowski

ISBN: 979-8-88814-257-8
1st Edition (1st printing, December 2024)
© 2024 Attabeira German de Turowski
All images © Attabeira German de Turowski
unless otherwise noted.

Rocky Nook Inc.
1010 B Street, Suite 350
San Rafael, CA 94901
USA

www.rockynook.com

Distributed in the UK and Europe by Publishers
Group UK
Distributed in the U.S. and all other territories by
Publishers Group West

TABLE OF CONTENTS

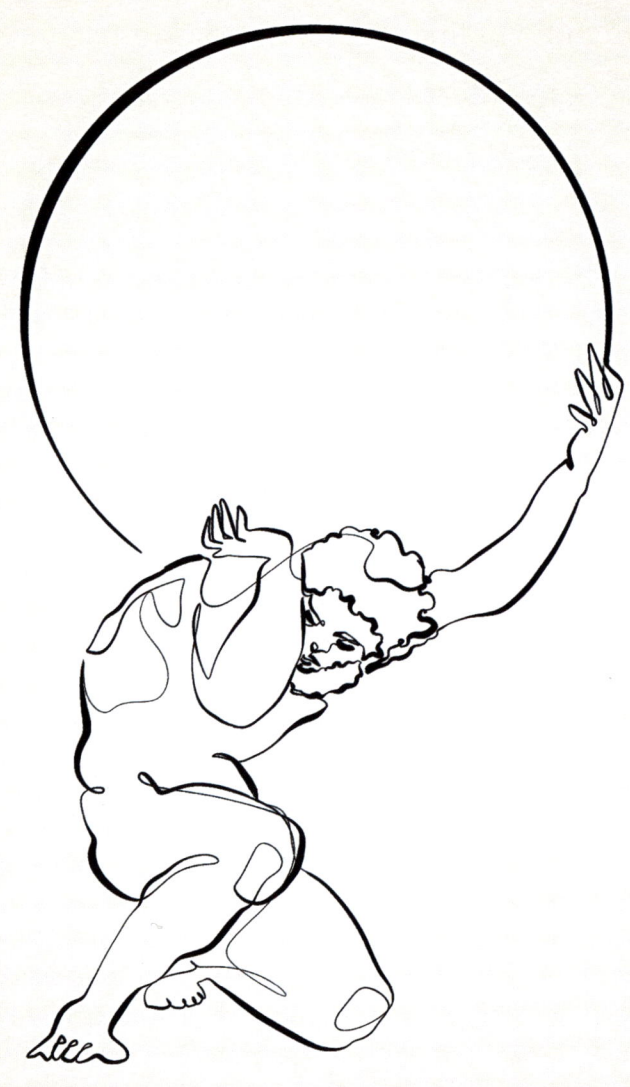

Introduction

I learned about one-line art as an adult. Growing up I took countless art lessons where I tried to master watercolors, painting with acrylics, and even anime. Unfortunately, all these art styles had some things in common that made it impossible for me to stick to them: They required time and resources. As I grew older, I was able to buy better paints and brushes, but finding time to be creative or to practice was harder than ever.

MY CREATIVITY WAS practically nonexistent at some point. Trying to get it back, I encountered one-line art in a book about short creative exercises for artistic confidence. The very first exercise was one about making a drawing without lifting the pencil from the paper: a one-line art challenge. My first attempt was far from art, but I could not stop myself from trying over and over. I felt something that day that I will never forget, I felt creative and satisfied with what I drew. Every single time.

One-line art was not only easy, it was convenient, too. Soon I was doing it in my agenda while on a call, on napkins while waiting for dinner, or on the back of receipts found in the depths of my purse. In my obsession I discovered that one-line art felt a lot like writing in cursive. It was a series of loops and lines that flowed together to gain meaning. Fast forward six years, over 10,000 students worldwide, and a one-line art illustrator reputation later, I can say with certainty that one-line art changed my life.

If you, like me, are on that quest for creativity, one-line art is a perfect way to start. I might have had some art training under my belt, but most of my students have zero background. They were just looking to find their artistic groove, whatever that looked like. Most of them wanted to learn one-line art because it is simple. Simple to learn, simple to practice, and simple to understand. Whether you've got an art degree or are picking up a pencil for the first time, one-line art meets you where you are, offering a friendly gateway into the world of creativity.

This book will teach you a comprehensive range of one-line art techniques, covering everything from the simplest form of freehand abstract one-line art to creating realistic depictions from references or muscle memory. Whether you prefer to work with traditional tools like pen and paper or explore the digital realm with apps like Procreate, you'll find guidance tailored to your preferences and level. Each section is packed with exercises carefully designed to help you master specific one-line art skills, providing a structured approach to your one-line art journey. So, whether you're just starting out or looking to refine your existing skills, this book has something valuable to offer at every step of the way.

If you know how to write, you already hold an advantage in your one-line art journey. One-line art, like writing, requires you to do penmanship-like drills that will get your hand used to the shapes and movements of the objects or subjects you desire to draw. Like writing, one-line art does not require fancy equipment or paper. So go ahead and dive into this book, after all you already possess the starting skills. If you can write, you can draw.

HOW TO USE THIS BOOK

MY 14 YEARS of teaching have taught me that people learn better by doing. Learning one-line art was of course no exception to that rule. The more I did it, the better my muscle memory became. Therefore, I've set out to make this book a workbook. It's not just about flipping pages and absorbing information passively. Instead, it's designed for active engagement, with hands-on exercises that will immerse you in the world of one-line art. Each chapter presents a new opportunity for you to roll up your sleeves and put pencil to paper.

You'll learn by doing exercises in each chapter. Rather than drowning you in theory or complex explanations, this book will go for a hands-on approach. Each exercise is carefully made to teach you a specific aspect of one-line art, whether it's mastering the steadiness of your line, line crossing and turning, or muscle memory.

All exercises are expected to be completed more than once, and on iteration as a cycle. Mastery doesn't happen overnight, and neither does mastering one's one-line art style. That's why these exercises are meant to be revisited, refined, and repeated. Each repetition brings you closer to perfection, honing your skills and deepening your understanding of this unique art form.

At the end of each skill-specific chapter, you'll find a "Chapter Recap" section. This serves as a quick way to refresh key points covered throughout the chapter. These recaps act as handy reference tools, allowing you to quickly locate important information or concepts without the need to search through the entire book. Additionally, they aid in self-assessing your work when practicing the exercises provided.

I suggest you do exercises in the order they appear in the book because they all lay the foundation for the exercises that will appear next. Think of it like building a house—you wouldn't start by putting up walls before laying the foundation. Similarly, each exercise in this book builds upon the previous one, providing a solid framework for your artistic journey.

All exercises can be done regardless of your level of expertise, as they all are made to fit into the abilities you have at the moment you do them. Whether you're a novice or a seasoned artist, there's something for everyone in these pages.

The exercises are designed to be adaptable, allowing you to progress at your own pace and tailor the learning experience to your current skill level.

There are also QR codes placed in certain sections of the digital online chapter of this book so that you can experience the exercises on an iPad in video form. In addition to the step-by-step instructions provided in the book, these QR codes offer another dimension to your learning experience. Simply scan the code with your smartphone or tablet, and you'll be able to watch video demonstrations of each exercise, providing even more guidance and support as you embark on your artistic journey.

MATERIALS

ONE OF THE most attractive features of one-line art is that the materials you use can vary greatly. The scope of materials you can use for this art style can range from a regular ballpoint pen over regular printer paper all the way to very expensive and sophisticated brushes and pens. In this section, we will explore what materials to use to achieve the results you want. Before I get into the materials though, it is important to note that you do not need to use these materials to learn or produce one-line art.

If you would like to get started right away, here's the basic set of materials I always have in my bag. This small set allows me to put in some practice whenever I'm stuck in line waiting somewhere or better yet, when inspiration strikes:

My go-to kit:
* HB pencil
* Sharpener
* Ballpoint pen
* Ink pen (I recommend a .01 point size)
* Pocket sketchbook (small for practicality)

Now let's move on to materials I use for specific purposes. The materials I mention below are solely to give you an idea of the possibilities and better clarity on which materials achieve what results.

HB pencil: HB pencils are the pencils one usually encounters in a classroom setting. They have a grayish-color finish, and they have a very particular texture to the line they produce. Due to the nature of the shape of their tip, the pencil can produce different widths depending on the angle they are held at. The closer the body of the pencil is to the paper, the wider and the lighter the line it will produce. When held up, the line won't vary regardless of the pressure applied to the pencil. Pencils are good training tools since they are erasable and allow us to correct mistakes while drawing.

Charcoal: Charcoal ranks among my favorite tools for one-line art due to its unique finish. It adds a rough texture to the artwork, adding depth and character. Similar to pencils, the width of a charcoal line can vary depending on how the charcoal is angled against the paper. However, unlike pencils, charcoal drawings are prone to smudging easily. To maintain the integrity of the drawing, it's essential to apply a charcoal-fixing spray or varnish to preserve it in its original state.

Ballpoint pen: One-line art crafted with a ballpoint pen maintains a consistent line width across the artwork, with only subtle variations based on pressure. While these variations may be imperceptible to the eye, they contribute to the overall texture and style of the piece. This tool excels in creating minimalistic and flat 2D-like one-line art, where uniformity is key to achieving the desired aesthetic. However, due to the limited influence of pressure on line width, it may not be the best choice for artwork requiring a sense of depth. In such cases, artists may find it challenging to convey the sense of 3D and perspective effectively.

Fine-tip pens and markers: Fine-tip pens and markers are labeled with a numbered size indicating the thickness of the lines they produce. Some are incredibly fine, even marked as .001, and can create lines as thin as a strand of hair. These pens are typically filled with ink or paint and are useful when you need precise line thickness in your drawing. The thinner the line, the smaller the details you can include in your artwork. However, like ballpoint pens, they are not suitable for creating depth in one-line art because they do not vary line thickness based on pressure. Instead, they provide a consistent line width throughout, ensuring steady and uniform strokes.

Brush pens/markers: Brush markers or pens are distinct from regular ones because they feature a brush tip rather than a standard pen or marker tip. Instead

of a fixed tip, they have a small brush at the end, giving illustrators the ability to control the width of the line. This feature allows artists to dynamically adjust the line width mid-stroke, offering greater flexibility and the opportunity to add depth to their drawings. By varying the thickness of the lines throughout their artwork, illustrators can create a sense of depth and dimensionality, enhancing the overall visual impact of their piece.

These three tools are grouped together in one section because they complement each other. In this book, there's a chapter dedicated to digital one line art. The Procreate app, in particular, offers features that breathe life into one-line art in ways traditional drawings can't. I specifically include iPads and iPad pens because, as of the writing of this book, Procreate is available only on iPads, and the app is optimized for use with Apple Pencil.

Brushes: Employing a traditional brush and paint for one-line art lends a distinctive texture and appeal to the artwork. The lines flow naturally, and depending on the shape of the brush, they can produce a diverse range of finishes. Some brushes change line thickness in response to pressure, while others maintain a consistent width. This versatility allows for artistic expression but requires more practice to control effectively. Additionally, brushes present challenges such as running out of paint or ink midline, making it difficult to create seamless one-line art pieces without lifting the brush or stopping the line.

Drip pens: Less commonly known, drip pens serve as excellent tools for creating larger-scale one-line art. Unlike traditional pens, they are tubes filled with paint and feature a mesh cover or roll-on ball instead of a tip. This unique design allows the paint to flow out as the pen is dragged across the paper. As a result, artists can seamlessly continue their lines without worrying about running out of ink or paint. However, drip pens do not vary in response to pressure, making them more suitable for situations where creating a sense of depth is not the primary goal.

Procreate app/iPad/Apple Pencil: These three tools are joined into one section because they work as one. In this book, there is a chapter in which we cover digital one-line art. The app Procreate specifically comes equipped with tools that make one-line art come alive in ways traditional one-line drawings don't. I have specifically added iPads and iPad pens here because, as of the writing of this book, the Procreate app has not made the app available for other tablets and stylus options.

These are just a few of the many tools available for line drawing, so don't feel limited by this list. Feel free to use any tools that you find comfortable or have on hand. It's important to remember that while these tools can enhance your artwork, they don't define it. Don't hesitate to experiment and learn with whatever tools you have access to. Ultimately, the tool you use won't affect how quickly or effectively you learn one-line art. What matters most is your dedication and practice.

SOFT SKILLS NEEDED FOR ONE-LINE ART

IN ADDITION TO mastering hard skills like creating one-line art without lifting the pencil, this book will also guide you in developing soft skills that can significantly enhance your artwork. These skills can be honed through practice, much like hard skills. The more you practice, the more proficient you'll become. Initially, you may need to consciously integrate these skills into your practice, but over time, they will seamlessly become a natural part of your one-line art process.

Here are the three main ones to practice and master:

Observation: Before beginning your piece, take a moment to observe your subject. Pay close attention to the details you want to emphasize. Consider the style of one-line art you envision for depicting these details. Take in the shapes and lines already present in your subject as you observe it/them. This initial observation will help you plan your approach and guide your artistic decisions as you create your one-line art. I often try to observe even when I am not drawing just so that I can use what I have stored in my memory later.

Memory: When you do not have anything to look at for a drawing, try remembering the shapes and details of objects and people you've looked at countless times. The people closest to you or everyday objects such as toothbrush and toothpaste. Try to observe them in your mind's eye the same way you'd observe something or someone that's there in the same space as you. Focus on the details you've seen many times before and try to convey that in your one-line art.

Imagination: I find this one to be the hardest. Once you've observed and memorized people and objects around you, the final step is to reimagine them as the things they could be or become. This is a very symbolic way to portray the things you observe and remember in order to portray them as one-line art.

Keep these soft skills in mind as you progress through this book. I'll be referring to them to connect them with the exercises and tasks you'll be undertaking in each chapter. This correlation will help you integrate these skills into your practice and enhance your overall one-line art journey.

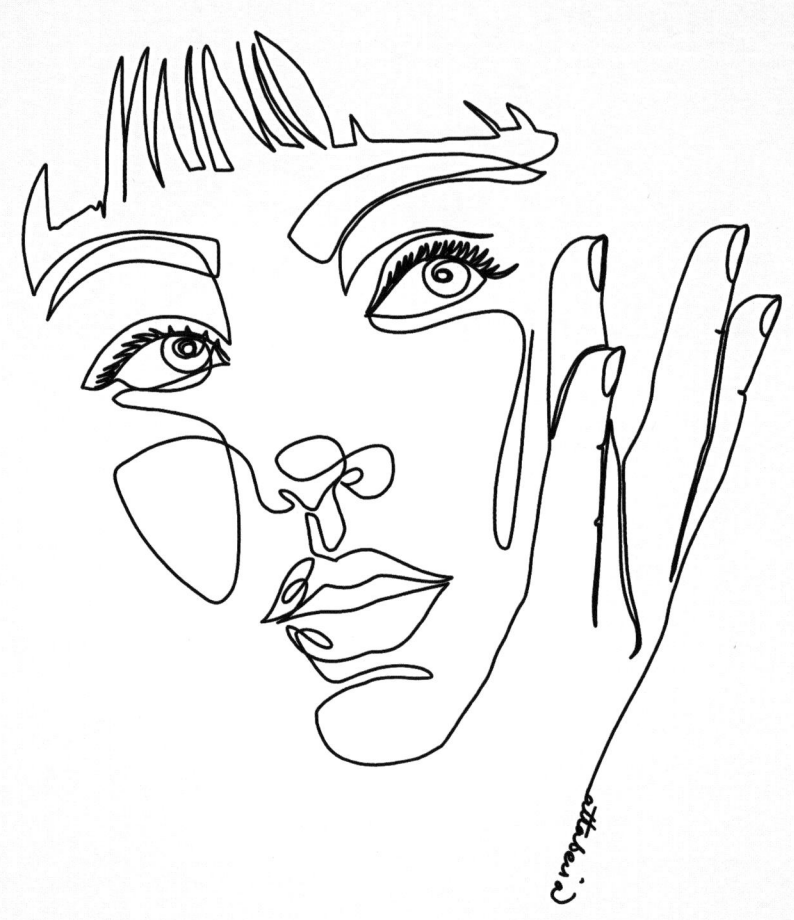

1

Building Muscle Memory

Just like any other muscles, hand muscles need to be warmed up before we start training them. The more we practice these exercises, the better our hands will know what to do and where to go. When warming up, it's important to focus on three main skills: line control, path redirection, and stroke stamina.

LINE CONTROL

AS YOU MAY have noticed, one-line art is very reliant on your ability to control the way your line looks and the way it moves. A single line done well can give you the illusion of distance, texture, and sometimes even shadows in a drawing. When working on a one-line drawing, using the line to give your drawing more detail is a skill that all one-line artists must learn to master. In this section, we will go through line control and certain line characteristics that can change the way your one-line art looks. We will also go through the exercises that you should be doing not only to be able to create these different types of lines, but also to know which one to use and when.

Before we get started, let's clarify some terms and definitions that will simplify the way we learn. These terms may be named differently in other books or other situations, but for the purpose of this particular lesson, we will adhere to these conventions in order to be able to learn these concepts swiftly.

Pulse: I like to call pulse the ability to draw a line with little to no shaking motion. I will refer to this as we're learning to create lines with a steady hand.

Flow: This term refers to when your line is drawn nonstop and seamlessly.

Line width: This term is pretty self-explanatory. It refers to how thick or thin your line is, and we will refer to it as we learn about depth in one-line art.

Lift: This is the act of lifting the pencil, pen, or bush to apply less pressure to the line.

Press: This term refers to the act of applying continuous pressure on the pencil, pen or brush as the line is drawn.

Simulating Distance in One-Line Art

To recreate the feeling of depth and distance in one-line art, we must imitate real life. If you take two exactly similar objects and place one far away and the other one closer to you, they will appear to have different sizes. One-line art tries to mimic this phenomenon by making the lines of the object that are supposed to be closer thicker and the lines of the object that appear to be farthest thinner in comparison. The brain takes this information and makes the viewer believe that the thinner line is, the farther away it seems to be. The same is true with the thicker lines. The thicker the line, the closer you'll believe the object to be.

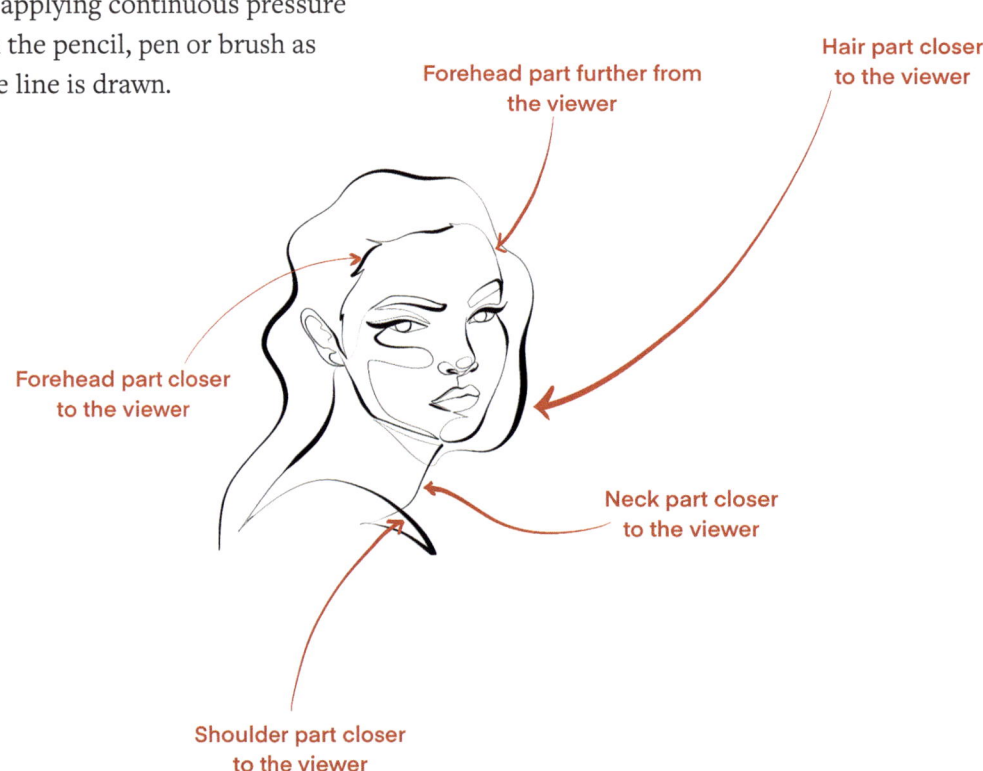

Forehead part further from the viewer

Hair part closer to the viewer

Forehead part closer to the viewer

Neck part closer to the viewer

Shoulder part closer to the viewer

Line Width to Focus or Distract the Viewer

Another important use of line width is applying the same-depth visual phenomenon to direct the viewer's attention to the lines you want others to see first. Thick lines are usually noticed first, whereas thinner lines are less noticeable. Notice how in the drawing below, some lines in the face are very thin. They are less important. The lines in the eyes, the hair, lips, and nose are more important and therefore thicker.

Other lines that are there for fill or for line continuation tend to be much thinner because they are not as important. The one-line artist wants these lines to be noticed later or barely noticed at all.

Achieving Thick and Thin Line Control When Drawing

When drawing in this style, being able to control the thickness of your line as you draw can be achieved with muscle control and practice. The ability to control the thickness of your line while drawing can be done by following simple line exercises. In these exercises, two things are important: pulse and flow.

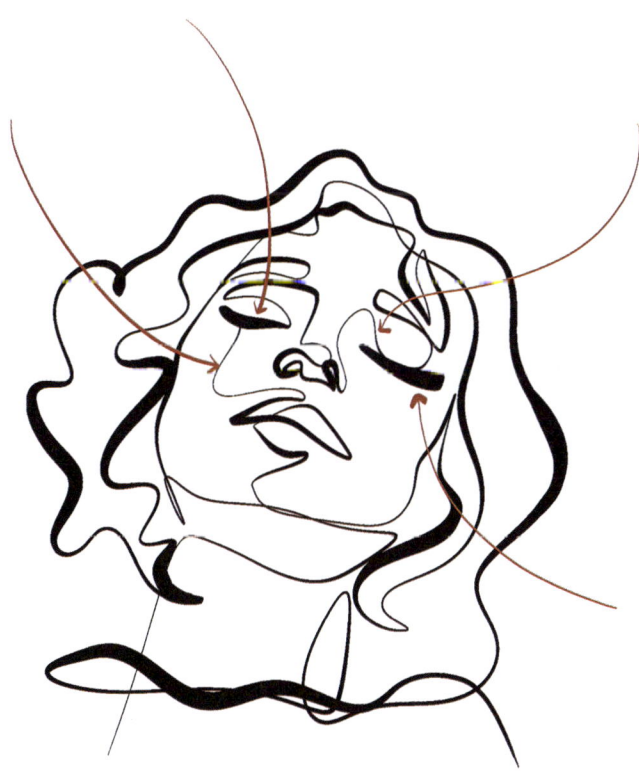

LINE-CONTROL EXERCISES

THE BEST WAY to improve line control is by doing line drills. Try to do these exercises without a shaky line and without stopping. The more you do the exercises, the better the lines will be. The exercises we will be doing for line control are very simple in nature and not very time-consuming. Do them whenever you get a chance with any tools you have at hand. Let's get right to them, shall we?

EXERCISE 1

Ups and Downs

This exercise helps with pulse and pressure control. It increases in difficulty depending on the tool you use for it. In other words, it will be fairly easy if you do it with a regular pencil or ballpoint pen, and harder with brush pens, brushes, and calligraphy equipment. This is because pencils and ballpoint pens have a hard tip, which helps keep your line steady. Brushes on the other hand, have the quality of movement and any tiny move from your hand will show up in your line. I recommend that you start off with a pencil and move on to more sensitive tools from there.

On a piece of paper start by drawing a line up and lift your wrist as you make the line from bottom to top. When you reach the height you desire, make a turn right and start going back down. When you do, apply pressure to make your line thicker/darker. Repeat. (See the example below.)

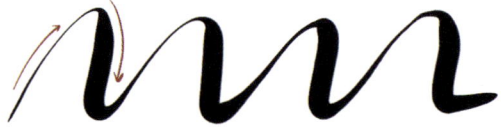

EXERCISE 2

Loops

This exercise helps with flow and pressure control. Just as in exercise 1, difficulty increases depending on the tool you use. Start with a pencil or a ballpoint pen and work up from there. On a piece of paper start by drawing a line up, and lift as you make a line from bottom to top. After doing so, make a turn right and start going back down. When you do, apply pressure to make your line thicker. When you reach the bottom again, make a loop before starting over again. (See the example below.)

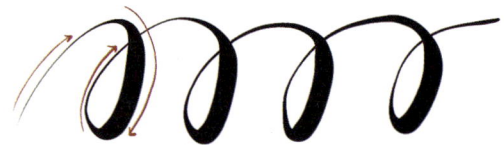

Curtains

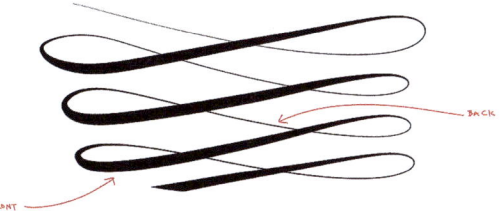

For your third exercise on line control, we will be doing something similar to exercises 1 and 2. Like the first two exercises, we will be lifting the pencil or brush when we want to make the lines that will be "behind," and then pressing down when we want to make the lines that will be in the front. Begin by making a diagonal line down, loop up and over, then repeat another diagonal line down in the same direction, but this time while pressing down so that it is thicker. (See the example below.)

Reminder: Thicker lines appear closer to the viewer, while thinner lines appear farther away from the viewer.

PATH REDIRECTION

WHEN CREATING ONE-LINE art, knowing how to approach the path your line will take is very important. One of the biggest challenges my students face is not knowing where to redirect their line. That's why I often practice loop styles and line redirection. These skills come in handy when tracing or using a photo as reference, because they help you continue when you think you've run out of places to take your line.

This is where loops, turnbacks, and shadow lining come into play! These three path redirection skills can help you be able to continue your line even if the contour of the object you're drawing is over.

Loops

Loops are the most common form of line redirection; they are also the most obvious ones, so they are the ones people tend to learn first. Whenever you try to do a one-line drawing, loops will allow you to move from one part of your drawing to another. They are also particularly useful

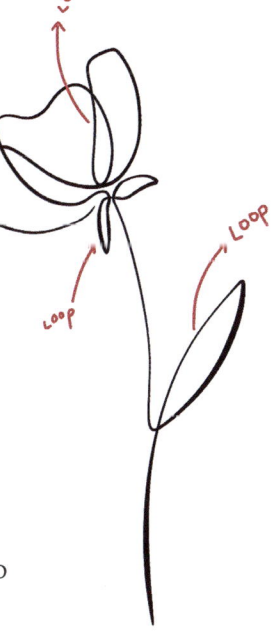

when trying to show the end of one section of an object and the beginning of another, all with just one line.

Turnbacks

Turnbacks are a little less common, but they are very useful when you have to return the way your line came without tracing the same line twice. Tracing over the same lines defeats the purpose of one-line art because the line cannot be followed by the observer. The clarity of the path you take with your line is what makes this art style interesting. When we turn back but use a separate returning line to frame the one already there, the result is something amazing.

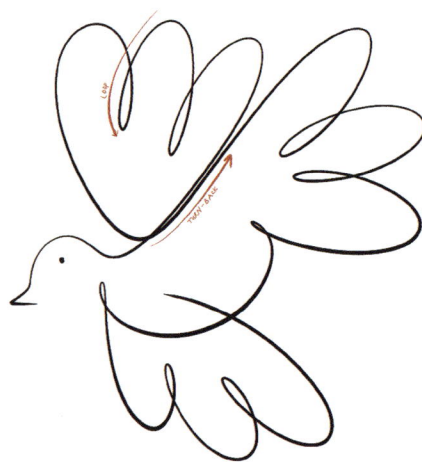

Shadow Lining

Shadow lining takes some practice, but they elevate the quality of your one-line art by a lot. Shadow lining focuses on finding new paths to your line by outlining

lowlights and highlights in what you're trying to draw. This technique makes your drawings look more sophisticated because it adds more detail and visual information to it, such as depth and hints into how the light would fall on the person or thing you're drawing. It is achieved by using thinner lines than the ones you use for your outline.

Important tip: Shadow lines must be subtle and not overdone. If overused, the drawing will look heavy and cluttered.

Redirecting the path your line takes is a skill all one-line artists should master. What's more, using a combination of loops, turnbacks, and shadow lining in your art will make sure that your drawings look varied and well balanced. Doing so consciously and purposely will elevate your one-line art.

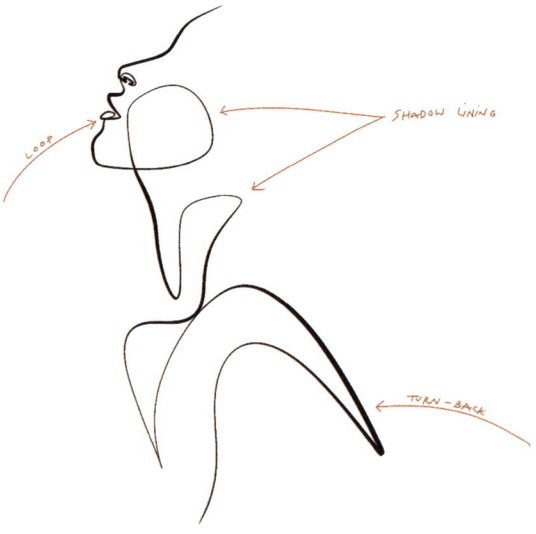

PATH REDIRECTION EXERCISES

Path Redirection

Try to make a one-line drawing of a flower four times. The flower must be simple and something you're used to drawing. It can be just the flower, no stem and no leaves. Attempt to do your line without lifting the pencil, and each time focus on one of the path redirection strategies you just learned. At the end, focus on combining two or three of the strategies to balance out your drawing.

The objective of this exercise is simply practicing path redirection. The drawing does not have to be perfect, or even pretty, we're simply showing our hand what to do when it does not know where to go.

Your exercise should be something like this:

LOOP

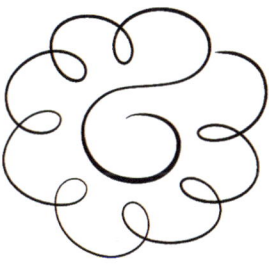

TURN-BACK

SHADOW LINING

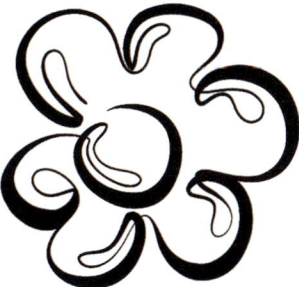

COMBINED

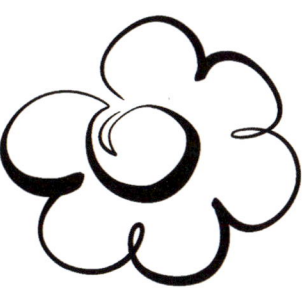

STROKE STAMINA

STROKE STAMINA HAS to do with how long you can carry your line without lifting your pencil. This is more of a vanity skill, but I think it is important to teach it in this book. There are several groups of one-line artists who believe that one-line art is not one-line art if the drawing was made with pauses in between. Others believe that the drawing being done in one continuous line would suffice. I am a firm believer that it really does not matter. Whether you are in the first group or in the second, one-line art is whatever you want it to be. I like to practice both styles for fun and use both styles interchangeably depending on my purpose is at the moment.

If I am creating a custom piece for a gift, like a portrait for a family member, I lift my pencil a thousand times because what is important to me at that moment is that my drawing looks exactly like the person I am trying to honor. On the other hand, when I am creating a free one-line drawing, where I am entertaining my friends or social media community, I will do it nonstop in one continuous line without ever lifting the pencil because my goal here is a show of skill as opposed to the final result. One technique focuses on the result, whereas the other focuses on the process.

THE PENCIL:
AN EXTENSION OF YOUR HAND

NOW THAT WE have made clear why learning stroke stamina is important, let us dive in how to actually do so. One of the most important parts of acquiring this skill is learning to hold the pencil and how to change the pencil position for comfort and mobility. I want you to think of the pencil as an extension of your hand and your hand as an extension of your arm. Acquiring stroke stamina requires you use your fingers, wrists, elbow, and sometimes even shoulders.

The more you get used to using your whole arm for drawing, the less tired your hand will get. The less tired you are, the more detailed your one-line drawing can be when drawing without lifting the pencil. Here are some finger, wrist, and arm moves you can try:

Finger movement

With the palm resting on the paper, the fingers move front and back in an extension and retraction movement.

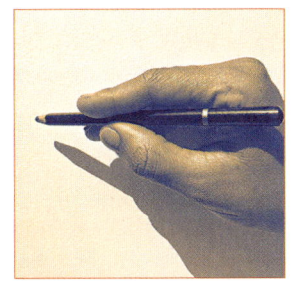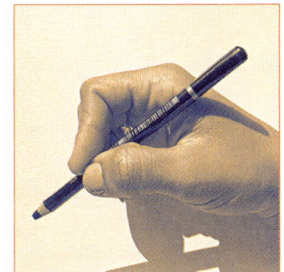

Wrist movement

With your elbow on the table, move your wrist up and down like so:

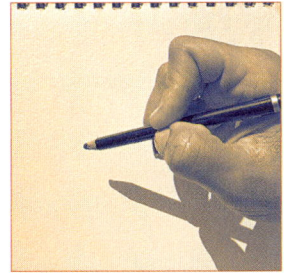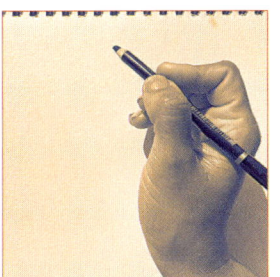

Elbow/arm movement

With your forearm touching the paper, the whole arm is engaged, moving up and down.

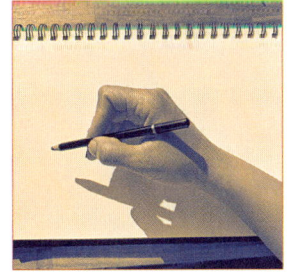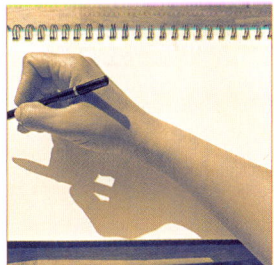

STROKE STAMINA EXERCISE

EXERCISE 5

Stroke Stamina

Fill up a paper with one single line. Try to not lift the pencil. If you do, start all over again on a new sheet of paper. Try to use all your moment points: fingers, wrist, elbow, and arm. I've done mine like so:

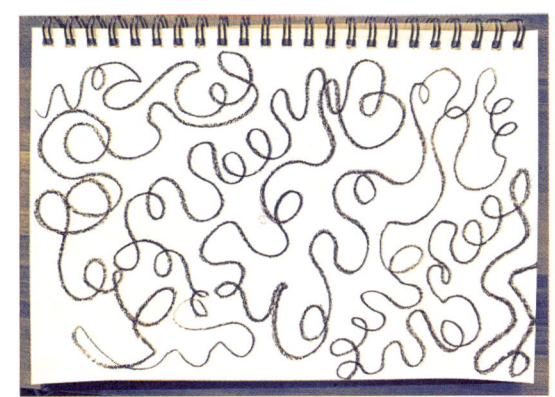

CHAPTER RECAP

JUST LIKE WARMING up before a workout, warming up hand muscles is crucial before diving into drawing. We highlighted three key skills: line control, path redirection, and stroke stamina.

Line control is essential for creating intricate one-line drawings. We discussed terms like pulse, flow, line width, lift, and press, which are crucial for mastering line work. Understanding these terms helps in creating detailed drawings and directing the viewer's attention within the artwork.

Simulating distance in one-line art is crucial for adding depth to drawings. By varying line thickness, artists can create the illusion of objects appearing closer or farther away, adding realism to their artwork.

Line width to focus or distract the viewer helps guide the viewer's gaze within the artwork. By adjusting line widths strategically, artists can emphasize important elements while subtly blending less significant details into the background.

Achieving thick and thin line control when drawing requires practice and muscle control. Through exercises like ups and downs, loops, and curtains, artists can improve their ability to manipulate line thickness and direction.

Path redirection is another vital skill in one-line artistry. Techniques like loops, turnbacks, and shadow lining help artists navigate the contours of their subjects seamlessly, adding complexity and depth to their artwork.

Path redirection exercises are a practical way to reinforce these techniques. By repeatedly drawing simple objects and focusing on different path redirection strategies, artists can enhance their muscle memory and proficiency in one-line drawing.

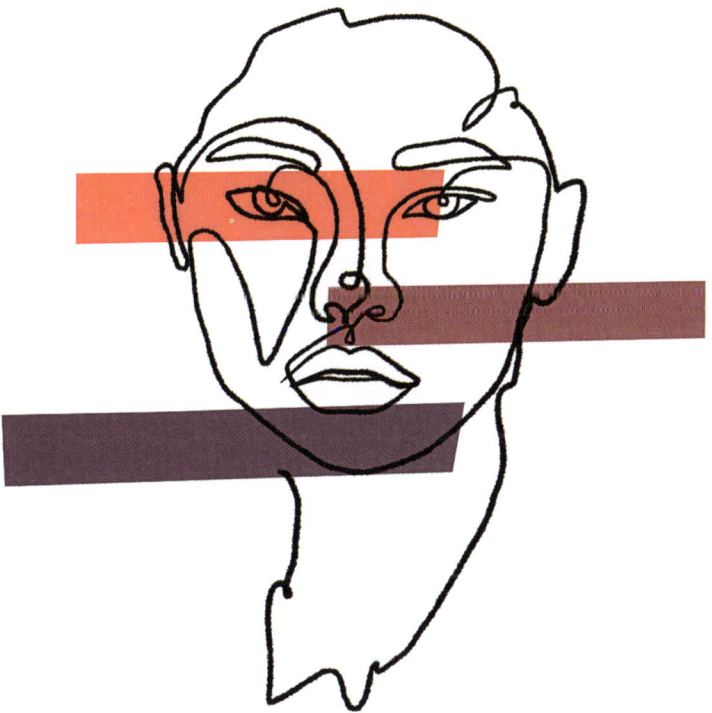

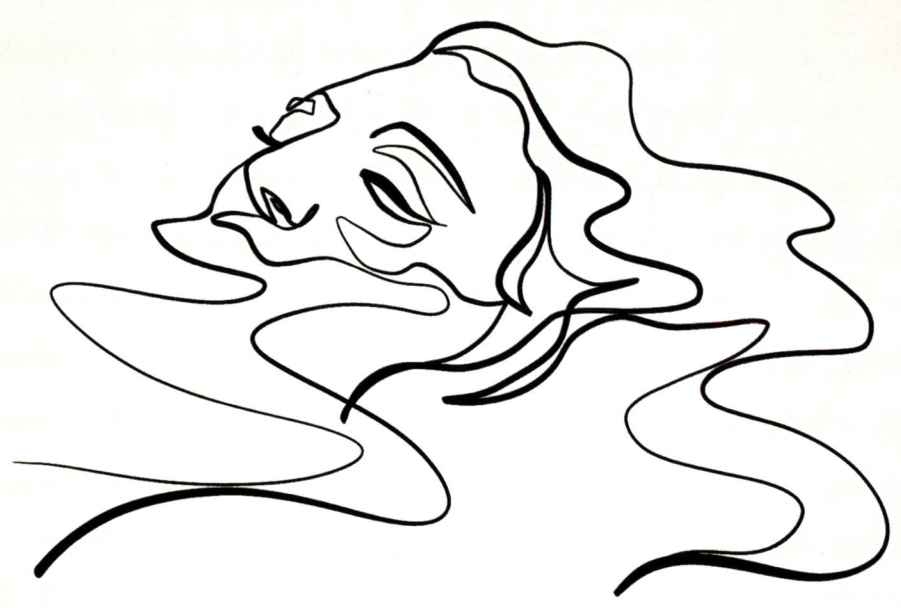

2

Abstract One-Line Art

One of the most popular styles of one-line art is abstract. The essence of one-line art lies in artistic expression through shapes that vaguely resemble known objects. Unlike realistic representation, one-line art offers creative freedom; it doesn't require precise likeness to real-life objects. For example, in abstract one-line art, a person's depiction might lack an eye, an ear, or have a peculiarly shaped head, yet still evoke the impression of a human head.

The allure of abstract one-line art lies in embracing the liberty to create with imagination rather than conforming to the constraints of reality.

To get started with our abstract one-line pieces there are certain concepts we need to go through before we begin drawing. These few concepts will get you in the right mindset before starting your exercises.

THE FREEDOM TO CREATE

UNDER THIS TITLE, I urge you to set aside any preconceived notions you may have about your skill level as a one-line artist. When it comes to abstract one-line art, technical knowledge of proportions, drawing techniques, or composition matters very little.

Instead, I encourage you to unleash your creativity and put your best (creative) foot forward as we delve into this section of the book. Toward the end of this chapter, I'll invite you to create some objects from memory. I encourage you to approach these tasks with freedom, relying on the mental images of those objects you hold in your mind's eye.

Decide Where the Focus of the Piece Goes

One of the fascinating aspects of creating one-line art is the freedom to determine the focal point of the piece. You have the autonomy to decide what can be omitted as less important, while also identifying essential elements that must be included. A good example of this is evident in abstract one-line portraits of incomplete faces.

Sometimes, only one eye is depicted, while other times, the nose and lips are left out entirely, leaving much to the imagination. This selective approach forces the viewer to focus on what is present rather than what is absent. Simultaneously, it invites the observer to fill in the gaps, allowing them to imagine the missing elements according to their preferences.

Abstract Does Not Always Mean Minimal

Many people assume that abstract one-line art, often featuring missing parts, is inherently minimalistic. There's a tendency to link omission with minimalism, assuming they always go hand in hand. However, abstract one-line art doesn't have to be minimal. In fact, it can be filled with detail and maximalism in what is chosen to be presented.

Consider the drawings in this chapter as examples. Both are instances of abstract one-line art, yet one is very minimalistic, while the other is the complete opposite. The complexity of your drawing depends on the number of lines you choose to use, while the style is defined by what is or isn't omitted.

DRAWING FROM MEMORY

DRAWING ONE-LINE ART is not just about capturing what we see; it's also about storing images in our memory and translating them onto paper. Everyday objects provide us with the perfect subjects to practice this skill, as they are familiar yet diverse in shape and complexity. The ability to draw from memory is a fundamental skill for any artist, enhancing observation, understanding of form, and the ability to abstract and simplify visual information.

Below you'll find a list of 15 prompts for you. Each prompt focuses on an object you likely encounter in your daily life. Through this exercise, you'll practice drawing these items using a single continuous line. This method encourages you to think critically about the essence of each object, improving your ability to recall and reproduce shapes and lines from memory.

Remember, the goal is not perfection but rather to develop a deeper connection with the visual world around you and to translate that connection into your art. So, feel free to use this list as a daily practice, an "Everyday object to draw" list, or as small everyday tasks to get better at one-line art.

Clock: Draw a classic analog clock as it strikes 10:10. Think about the circular shape and the positions of the hands.

Glass of water: Visualize a simple glass of water. Concentrate on the outline of the glass and the water level.

Bike: Capture the form of a bicycle, focusing on its two wheels, frame, and handlebars.

Pencil: Think about the shape of a traditional pencil, including its pointed tip and eraser end.

Apple: Draw an apple, starting from its top near the stem, circling around to define its round shape.

Eyeglasses: Depict a pair of eyeglasses, concentrating on the frame and the circles of the lenses.

Book: Illustrate an open book, emphasizing the curve of its spine and the outline of its pages.

Newspaper: Sketch a newspaper, folded in half, with the creases and outline of its pages.

Diary: Draw a closed diary or journal, starting with its spine and around to its edges.

Flower: Visualize a simple flower, such as a tulip, focusing on its stem, leaves, and petal outline.

Mobile phone: Capture the basic shape of a mobile phone, including its rectangular form and the screen.

Cushion: Sketch a cushion or pillow, paying attention to its fluffy outline and corners.

Mug: Depict a mug, concentrating on its handle and the curve of its opening.

Lamp: Draw a table lamp, including its base, stem, and the shape of the lampshade.

Shoe: Visualize a shoe, starting from its opening to the toe and around the sole.

ABSTRACT ONE-LINE PORTRAITS

Reimagining the Human Face

Abstract one-line portraits heavily rely on your ability to recall facial expressions and features from memory. They are commonly featured in fine-art settings, such as paintings exhibited in galleries. These portraits often capture a feeling rather than depicting a specific person, with little regard for precise facial dimensions or human anatomy measurements.

In abstract one-line portraits, there's artistic license to exaggerate or minimize facial features, sometimes resulting in a cartoonish appearance. The magic of this portrait style lies in observing your source of inspiration, whether it's a live model, a photograph, or a video, and feeling the freedom to deconstruct their "likeness" to create an abstract portrait.

Creating an Abstract One-Line Piece

Now that you have a clearer understanding of what abstract art entails, let's dive into some exercises to put it into practice. We'll explore various scenarios, each focusing on a different skill within abstract one-line art. Toward the end, we'll tackle a final task that's more open-ended, allowing you the freedom to approach the drawing in whichever way your observation and imagination lead you.

ABSTRACT PORTRAITS EXERCISES

Abstract One-Line Portrait

For this initial exercise, let's create your first one-line portrait. We'll begin by drawing from memory. Consider the essential elements of a face: the eyes, nose, mouth, ears, and perhaps the hair surrounding the face. Without lifting your pencil, attempt to sketch several faces. Below are some examples to get you started, but feel free to generate additional versions using your own imaginative process:

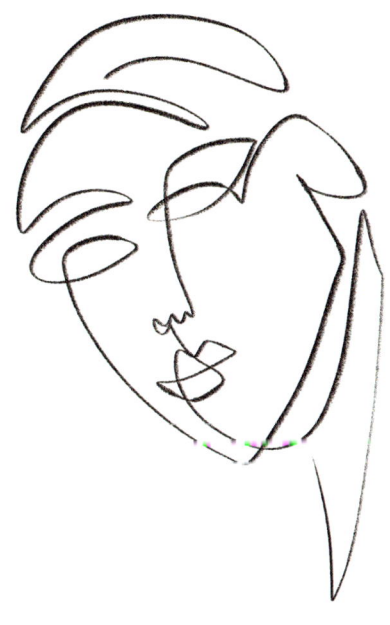

EXERCISE 7

Abstract One-Line Portrait of a Woman

For this second exercise, let's draw from memory once more, but this time, let's aim to create a portrait that is clearly feminine. Think about the details, traits, or characteristics that typically convey femininity. Perhaps it's long, flowy hair, or maybe it's long eyelashes and winged eyeliner. You decide what elements to include. Your focus for this abstract piece is to ensure that your subject is unmistakably female. Remember, we're creating portraits, so

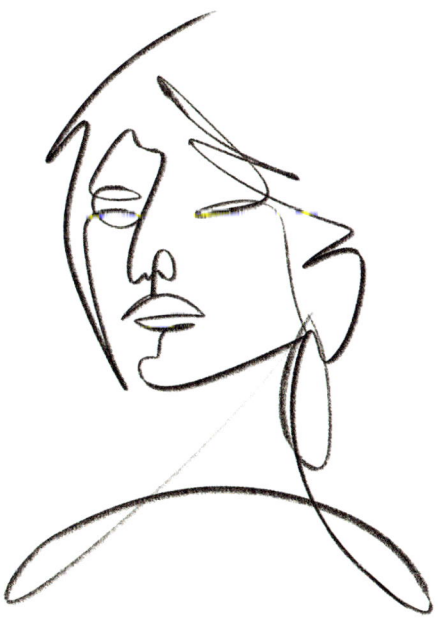

pay attention to the eyes, nose, mouth, hair, or even the top of the shoulders.

Keep in mind that your drawing doesn't have to be minimalistic; it just needs to be abstract. So, feel free to add details that will enhance the feminine look of your art, regardless of whether it's minimalistic or not. I've done mine for reference on the previous page.

EXERCISE 8

Abstract One-Line Portrait of a Man

For this third exercise, let's draw from memory once again, but this time, our goal is to create a portrait that is obviously masculine. Think about the details, traits, or characteristics commonly associated with masculinity. It could be a strong jawline, a more angular nose, or perhaps facial hair. You decide which

elements to include. Your focus for this abstract piece is to ensure that your subject is clearly male. Remember, we're still creating portraits, so pay attention to the eyes, nose, mouth, hair, and other defining features typically found in male faces. Here is my example:

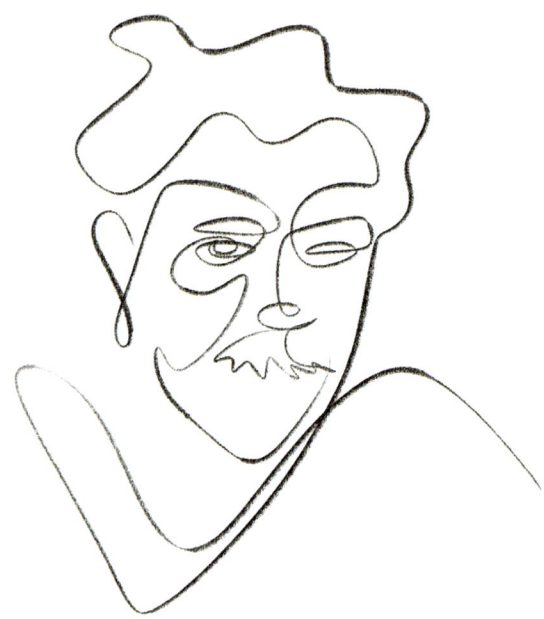

ABSTRACT ONE-LINE ANIMALS

ABSTRACT ONE-LINE ANIMALS are fun and unexpected drawings of animals we easily remember. This style of art simplifies the recognizable features of animals, making them easy to understand in a playful and straightforward way. As with portraits, abstract one-line animal art focuses on these familiar features. For example, when drawing a camel, it's

important to show its humps, and when drawing a lion, don't forget its majestic mane.

Drawing animals can be a bit trickier than human portraits because we don't encounter them as frequently as human faces. As a result, when drawing them from memory, we may struggle to remember beyond the features that make them recognizable, like humps or a mane. However, this is where creativity and imagination come in handy. Since our drawings are abstract, we have the freedom to fill in the blanks whenever our memory falls short.

The Power of Perspective and Detail

Another way to enhance your abstract one-line drawing of an animal when your memory fails you is by experimenting with a new perspective and incorporating additional details. Once you've identified a distinctive feature for your subject, consider varying the angle from which you draw the animal. Are you viewing it from the side or from above? Imagine your viewpoint as that of a camera—how would the animal be positioned?

When it comes to adding detail, I always like to start with the most obvious and simple shape my memory can recall of that animal and then I make several versions of the same animal in the same position. But every time I do it, I think of more detail I can add in my line.

Please don't hesitate to add detail to your line; it will greatly enrich your drawing. I've mentioned this before, and I'll continue to emphasize it throughout the book: Abstract art doesn't always have to be minimal.

ABSTRACT ANIMALS EXERCISES

Adding Detail

For our initial animal exercise, let's practice adding detail to a one-line drawing of a jellyfish. As mentioned earlier, we'll begin with simplicity. We'll draw the jellyfish as we remember or imagine it and repeat this process several times. With each iteration, focus on enhancing a specific area of the subject, striving to make each version an improvement or a variation of the details in the last ones.

I've completed four iterations of the jellyfish exercise. In my first version, I kept it simple with just a semicircle and wavy tentacles below it, representing the basic shape of the jellyfish. Moving to the second iteration, I added some shine to the top part of the jellyfish to give it more depth and dimension. The third iteration saw me adding texture to the tentacles by altering the stroke style. Finally, in the fourth iteration, I included an oval at the base of the jellyfish to create a more cylindrical appearance. Each iteration is valid and abstract in its own right.

Now it's your turn to add detail to each iteration of your drawing, whether it's the jellyfish or another animal of your choosing.

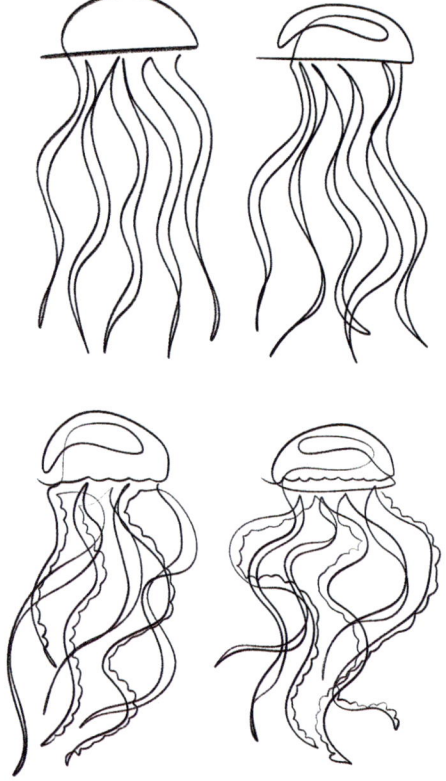

Adding Detail and Perspective

Exercise 2 combines detail and perspective. For this exercise, I'll revisit the first one with a butterfly instead of a jellyfish. I'll create two iterations focusing on adding detail. Then, for the third iteration, I'll change the position of the butterfly to a profile view rather than a front, open-winged one.

On my first iteration, I make a very basic version of the butterfly. It's almost childlike and has very simple wings and antennae. On my second iteration, I try to add the detail of the pattern on the wings with my line. On the third and last iteration, as you can see, I keep the improvements of my second butterfly but change its position to change it up a bit.

ABSTRACT ONE-LINE BOTANICALS

FLORAL ONE-LINE ART is probably one of the most popular themes with one-line art style. There is something soothing about following a simple line twisted into a tulip or a rose. Flowers, leaves, and plants make wonderful one-line art motifs for decor, stationary design, and even tattoos.

When creating abstract florals, the techniques we've explored in this chapter remain relevant. Developing our abstract one-line flower skills allows us to consolidate all the strategies we've learned, bringing together and applying all the elements of abstract art. While we've previously approached these steps separately, now we'll attempt to integrate them more seamlessly. This means some of these steps will begin to occur simultaneously, enhancing our overall artistic process.

ABSTRACT BOTANICAL EXERCISES

EXERCISE 11

Abstract One-Line Tulip

Let's consider drawing a tulip. The initial step involves recalling what a tulip looks like. Take a moment to visualize its shape, parts, and details. Begin with the first iteration, where you create a simple set of 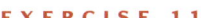 basic shapes connected by a continuous line. With each subsequent iteration, recall the image of a tulip in your mind's eye and add any details that make it distinct. Gradually add more detail or consider changing perspective as you see fit.

I have done this exercise for the tulip.

Now it's your turn. Choose a simple tulip or a flower you know or remember. Make as many iterations as you need, but try any variation of this progression:

* Remember, make simple shapes

* Remember, add detail and distinctive features

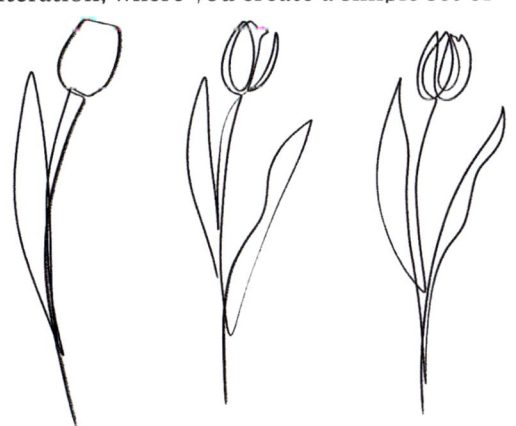

* Remember, add more detail   * Imagine what you can't remember

JUDGING YOUR WORK

BEFORE DELVING INTO more complex one-line art, it's crucial to acknowledge that treating your one-line journey as a process will enhance your enjoyment. Don't expect to become a one-line guru overnight—it's a journey, as I mentioned earlier. Every stage of your work is worthy of admiration because with each attempt, you learn something new. Even if a piece feels like a failure, you've gained insight into what not to do. Every piece you create brings you closer to your goal, acting as a step forward. The more steps you take, the closer you'll get to achieving your ideal one-line drawing skills.

Weird pieces of one-line art may still arise, even after years of practice—I've experienced this firsthand. Feeling dissatisfied with your work from time to time is something that, in my opinion, never completely disappears. Therefore, it's essential to speak to yourself kindly and view every piece you produce as an opportunity for self-examination. Focus on the details to pinpoint what bothers you, what you like and want to keep the same, and what you can improve upon next time. This approach will help you grow as an artist and continue to refine your skills.

CHAPTER RECAP

ABSTRACT ONE-LINE ART offers a creative departure from realistic representation, providing artists with the freedom to express themselves through shapes that loosely resemble known objects.

Focus on the freedom to create to set aside any preconceived notions about your skill level. Technical proficiency matters little in abstract one-line art; instead, creativity and imagination take precedence.

Deciding where the focus of the piece goes allows artists to determine the focal point of their artwork, selectively omitting less important elements while emphasizing essential features. This approach invites viewers to engage with the artwork by filling in the gaps with their imagination.

"Abstract does not always mean minimal" is a statement to challenge the assumption that abstract art is inherently minimalistic. Abstract one-line art can be filled with detail and maximalism, depending on the artist's choice of lines and omissions.

Memory drawing highlights the significance of drawing from memory in developing an artist's ability to abstract and simplify visual information. This section stresses the value of practicing with everyday objects to enhance an artist's memory recall and their capacity to distill complex forms into simpler abstract representations.

Abstract one-line portraits and abstract one-line animals were explored as specific applications of abstract one-line art. These exercises provided opportunities to practice recalling and simplifying familiar subjects, such as faces and animals, from memory.

Judging your work is an essential aspect of the artistic process. Remember to view each piece as a step forward in your journey, recognizing that growth comes from self-examination and continuous practice.

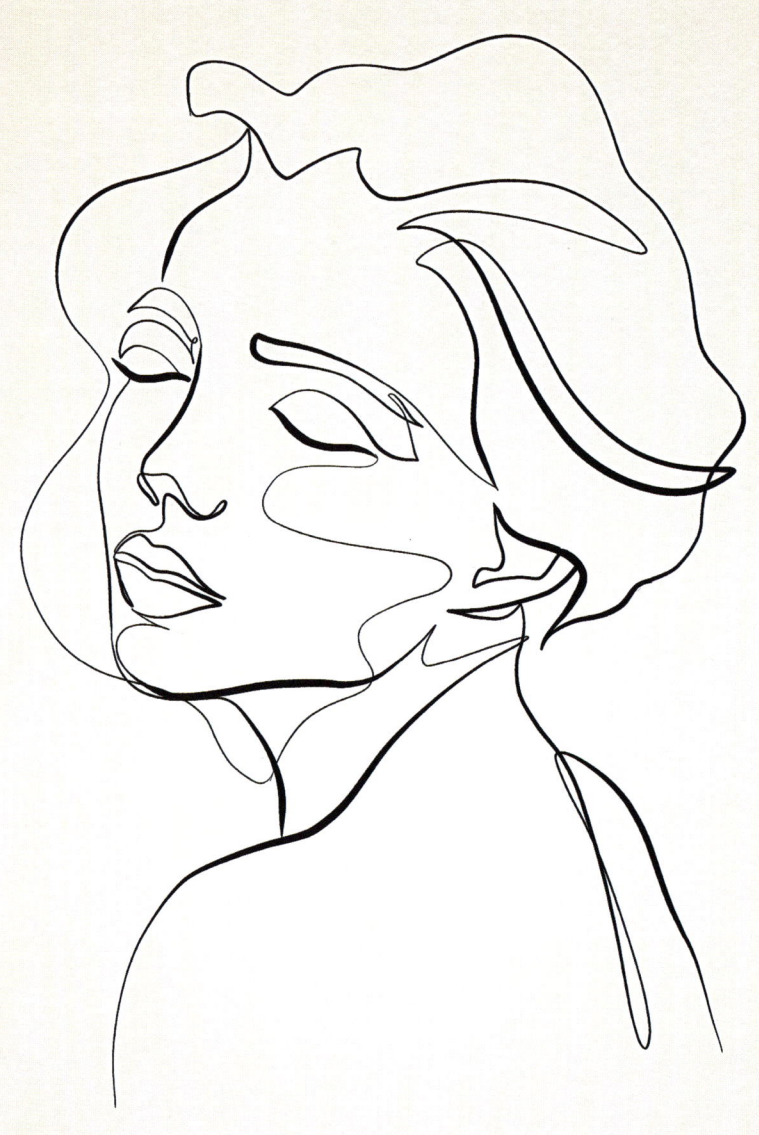

3

Realistic One-Line Art

Now we're transitioning to creating more accurate depictions of the subjects or objects we want to draw. This approach is known as realistic one-line art, and mastering it typically requires more practice than abstract one-line art. Fortunately, there are numerous strategies to help improve your skills in realistic one-line art. Practice and consistency are key to ensuring that the skills you acquire along the way remain sharp over time.

Due to the complexity of realistic one-line art, this chapter will concentrate solely on realistic portraits. This focus allows us to cover all the components that comprise this fascinating branch of one-line art. However, this doesn't imply that the skills you'll learn here can't be applied to realistic one-line drawings of plants and animals. Feel free to use the techniques and insights gained from portraits when attempting to depict animals and plants as realistically as well.

REALISTIC PORTRAITS

Making One-Line Art Look Real

In one-line art, using just one simple line to show depth and make things look real is quite the task. Imagine how light plays on objects and how shadows form. Where the light hits, your lines should be thin and light. Where there are shadows, make your lines thicker. This trick helps give your drawing a 3D feel on a flat surface.

Try looking at objects around you under different lighting. See how shadows change and how light shapes objects. In your drawings, use thicker lines for deeper shadows and thinner lines where the light is strongest. Remember, your lines are not just lines—they tell a story of how light dances around your subject.

The Basics of Drawing Faces and Bodies

To make your drawings of faces look real, start with some basic know-how about human shapes. You don't need to know every detail, but getting the big parts right helps a lot.

There's a simple rule that eyes are about one eye-width apart, and that the nose lines up with the

earlobes. When you draw faces, think about where the jawline, eyes, mouth, and nose go. You don't need to draw every detail, but getting these parts in the right place makes a big difference.

Using Guidelines

Another important skill we'll need to improve in our one-line art realistic portraits is using lines to guide us when placing the eyes, nose, and mouth on our subject's face. Many portrait artists use these lines, often referred to as "construction lines." Fortunately, for creating a one-line portrait, we only need the basic guidelines of a face. Be sure to create these guidelines lightly with a pencil so they can be easily erased later.

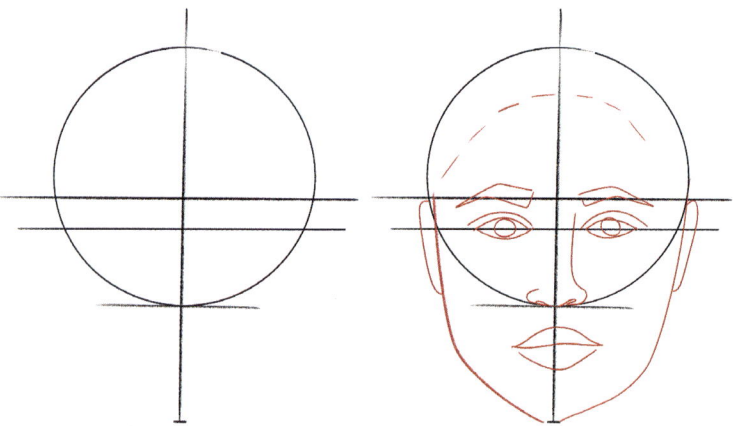

One of the simplest ways to start a front-facing one-line portrait is by creating guidelines consisting of a circle for the head, a vertical line down the middle extending beyond the circle's limits to mark the chin's end, and three horizontal lines to indicate the eyes and eyebrows, as shown in the drawing below.

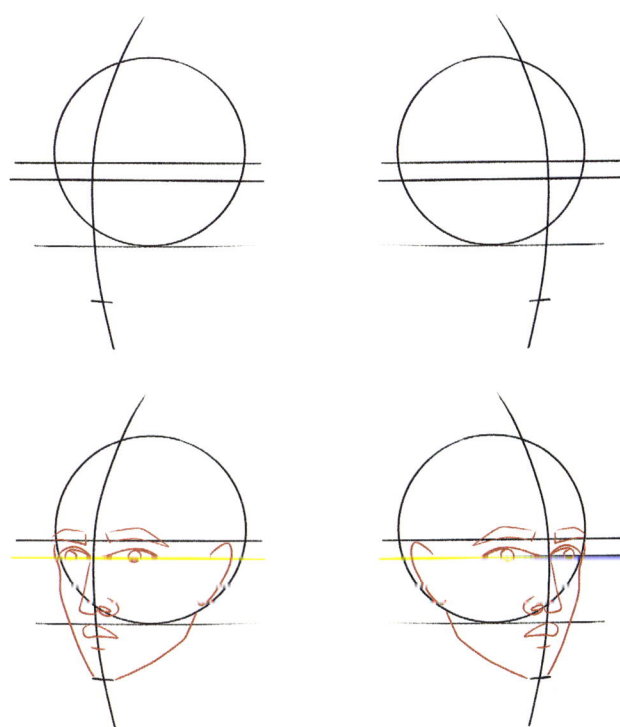

Guidelines for Other Positions

Front-facing facial guidelines are the easiest to create because we are naturally more adept at symmetry. There's a familiarity to a face looking straight ahead, requiring minimal adjustment as long as the eyes and eyebrows are similar in size and the nose and mouth are centered. However, you can create guidelines for other positions by adjusting these lines slightly. In the drawing below, notice how shifting the center line off-center allows for guidelines for more dynamic positions that aren't perfectly centered.

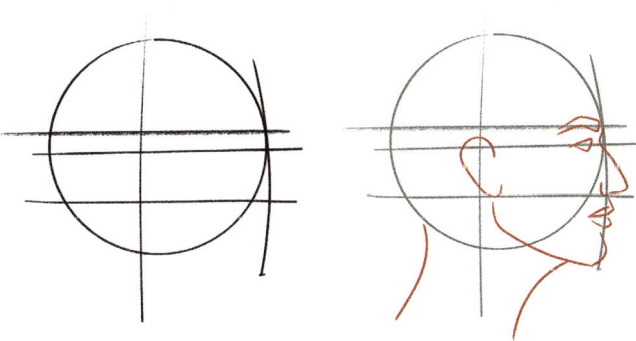

Another option is a full-profile guideline, which differs slightly from the front and three-quarter facing ones but is equally valuable to learn. Although it requires a few more lines, I've included a step-by-step diagram to illustrate its structure. Keep in mind that if it doesn't look perfect on your initial attempts, practice will help you refine it over time.

GUIDELINES EXERCISES

EXERCISE 12

A Front-Facing One-Line Portrait

Using guidelines, draw a one-line portrait of a person. Who you draw is your choice, it doesn't have to be someone real; the point is simply to follow the guides you've set up for yourself. Remember to make your guide in pencil and make your stroke light so that you can erase your guideline later. When you feel satisfied with your guidelines, draw your one line over it in pen. You can decide whether to do it without lifting up the pen or not.

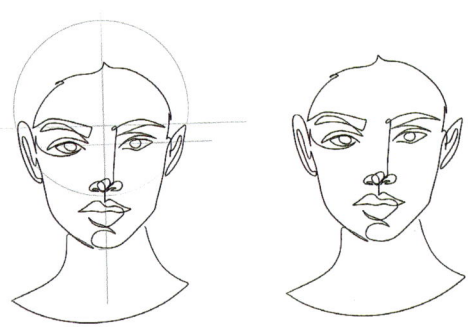

EXERCISE 13

A Three-Quarter-Facing One-Line Portrait

Using a side-view guideline, draw a one-line portrait of a person. Once more, who you draw is your choice and, like last

time, follow the guides you've set up for yourself. Make your guide in pencil and your one-line over it in pen. This time around, practice making it in one go without lifting the pencil.

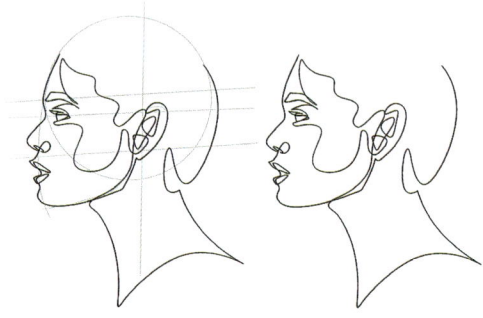

EXERCISE 14

A Profile One-Line Portrait

With your profile guide in hand, attempt to create a one-line portrait using the same approach you used with the front-facing and three-quarter views. Don't be discouraged if it appears a bit off, as side profiles can be challenging. Below, I've provided my attempt as well.

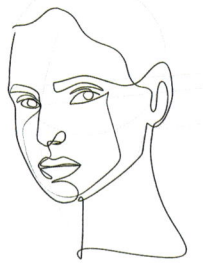
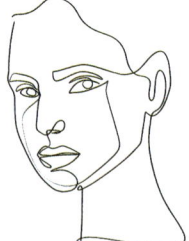

IMPROVING YOUR PORTRAITS

Adding Expression and Feeling

Another technique to elevate your one-line art is by incorporating facial expressions that reveal something about your subject. A slight smile or furrowed brow can convey a wealth of emotion in a portrait. Even subtle details like positioning the pupils slightly to the side and upward, as if the subject is wondering about something, can add depth to the artwork. These nuances allow the subject to tell a story, convey a message, or evoke an emotional response from the viewer.

Adding expressions into your one-line art can be challenging, so it's crucial to incorporate the intended emotion into your guidelines before starting your line. The eyes, eyebrows, and mouth are the primary indicators of expressions, as they have the most range in movement.

By adjusting these features in your guide, you'll get a better idea of how your final one-line portrait will end up looking. Below are some examples of drawings with the guideline I used and the result I got.

Using Varied Physical Traits

One reason I love one-line art portraits, and why they're my favorite style, is because of the limitless possibilities they offer when drawing people. I'm endlessly fascinated by individuals and their unique features. There's an abundance of characteristics to consider capturing, and even more that I might not have considered yet due to the sheer variety of options available. Despite having completed over 500 portrait commissions, I still encounter new facial features to draw that I've never tackled before.

Changing up physical traits helps keep you as an artist on your toes and your work fresh. The more you change up your features, the more well-rounded you become as a one-line art portrait maker.

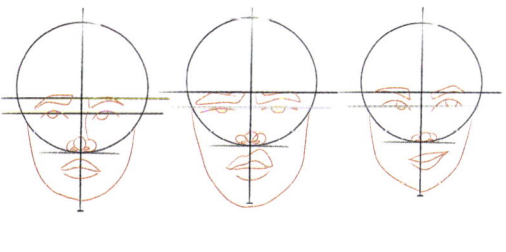

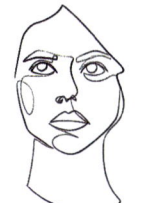 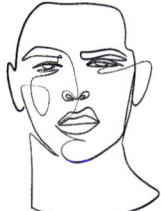 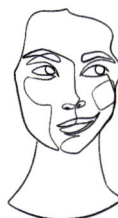   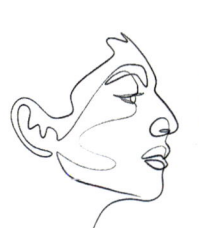 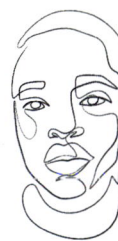 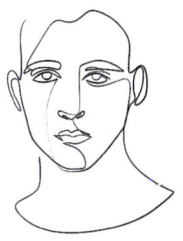

With each iteration think of what this subject can have that you would like to try. Do they have a beard? Freckles? Hooded eyes or a Greek-goddess nose? The more adventurous you get with your subjects, the more comfortable you'll feel when it is time to draw someone with very recognizable facial features.

Simulating Texture in Your Line

In a portrait, one of the most textured features is hair. Whether abundant or sparse, hair significantly influences a person's appearance, often being the most memorable characteristic for some. Unlike skin, which varies in shades and contours, hair poses a unique challenge in one-line art due to its diverse textures and styles.

Adding texture to your line is entirely achievable by adjusting the stroke of your line. For instance, irregularly swirly strokes can depict curly hair, while thick and thin curves can represent wavy hair. Similarly, sharp, straight strokes can convey the texture of straight hair. These techniques offer ways to incorporate additional detail and uniqueness into your one-line portraits.

Adding Depth

My preferred method for enhancing the realism of my one-line portraits is by adjusting the thickness of my lines to create the illusion of depth. I make certain lines thicker to appear closer to the viewer's eye, while thinner lines recede into the background. This technique requires practice and mastery of pressure and stroke control. By consistently practicing the exercises covered earlier in this book, you'll gradually improve your ability to execute this technique effectively.

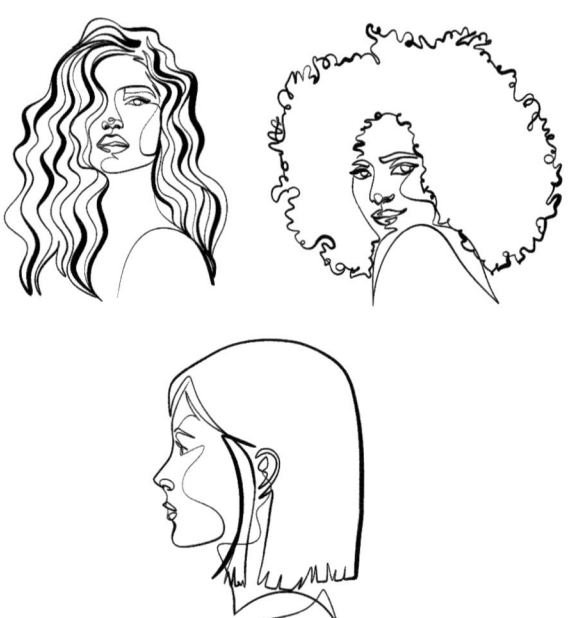

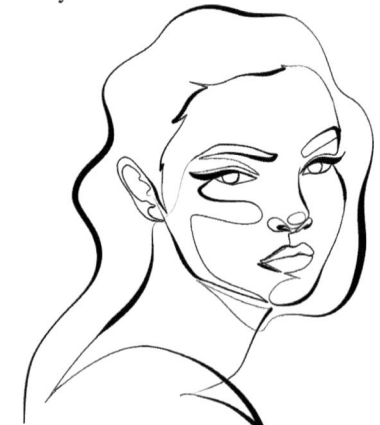

To begin mastering this technique, focus on making the connection lines thin and the feature lines thick. For instance, when drawing the eyes, mouth, nose, and eyebrows, aim for slightly thicker lines. In contrast, the segments that connect these features, such as those passing through the cheek or jawline, should be thinner. This approach helps create a sense of depth and dimensionality in your one-line portraits.

Planning Your Drawing

Before diving into the exercises in this section, it's essential to clarify that adding expression to your one-line drawing happens during the guideline sketching phase. The positioning of the eyebrows, eyes, and mouth should be incorporated into your initial sketch. Conversely, incorporating physical traits, texture, and depth occurs as you create your one-line art with a pen over your guidelines. Remember to keep this distinction in mind as you tackle the upcoming tasks based on the concepts we've just covered.

IMPROVING PORTRAITS EXERCISES

EXERCISE 15

Adding Expression

For this exercise, create another front-facing one-line portrait guideline. Focus solely on the guideline—no one-line art yet. This time, aim to change the expression from a neutral one to one of the emotions listed below. When you have the guidelines made and you're satisfied with your chosen emotion, feel free to move on to one-lining.

I've opted to depict happiness, but feel free to choose any of the four emotions provided to complete this task.

Emotions to choose from:

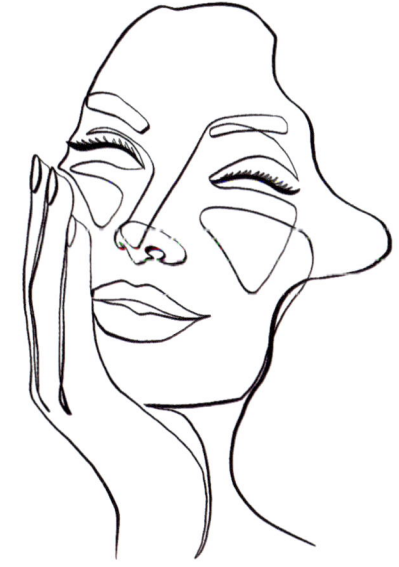

* Happiness   * Curiosity
* Sadness   * Surprise

Adding Physical Traits and Simulating Texture

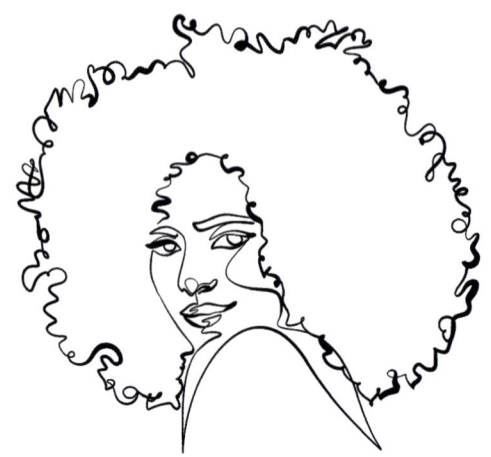

Now that you've created the guidelines for the expression task, take a moment to plan the physical traits of your subject. Consider factors like hair type or style, the shape of the eyes, lips, and nose.

Once you've made your decisions, proceed to complete your one-line drawing over the guidelines you created earlier. When drawing the hair, apply the stroke strategies for texture that we've learned in this chapter. This will help make the hair look more realistic and therefore make your drawing more striking.

Adding Depth

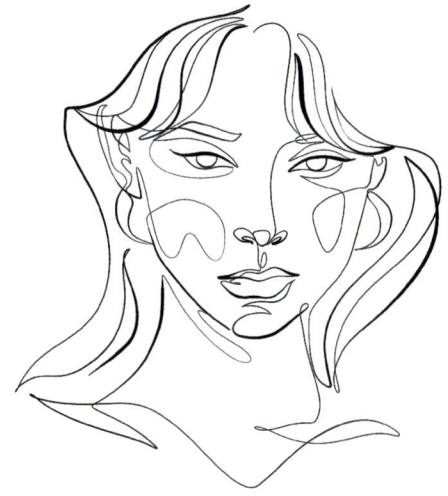

For the final task in this chapter, create another realistic one-line piece from start to finish. Begin by sketching the guidelines for your portrait, incorporating any desired expressions or physical traits. Then, proceed to complete your one-line drawing, making sure to add depth to your lines as discussed earlier. Feel free to experiment with other improvements from our list as well. Remember, apart from adding depth, the creative choices are entirely up to you. I've done mine like this:

CHAPTER RECAP

Transition to realism: Realistic one-line art offers a departure from abstract representations, requiring more practice and precision. Mastery in this style demands dedication and consistency over time.

Focus on portraits: This section concentrates solely on drawing realistic portraits, thoroughly covering the techniques necessary for mastering this style. The skills learned can also be applied to drawing plants and animals realistically.

Light and shadow: Using line thickness to represent light and shadow is a critical technique for adding depth and realism. Thicker lines suggest shadows, while thinner lines indicate areas illuminated by light.

Drawing faces basics: A foundational knowledge on human anatomy emphasizes the importance of accurate placement of eyes, nose, mouth, and jawline for creating realistic facial drawings.

Using guidelines: Guidelines play a crucial role in creating realistic portraits. By sketching basic lines to mark the placement of facial features, artists can ensure accuracy and proportion in their artwork.

Expressive portraits: Incorporating emotions and facial expressions adds depth and character to one-line portraits.

By adjusting the positioning of features during the guideline-sketching phase, artists can convey various emotions effectively.

Varied physical traits: Realistic one-line portraits thrive on diversity. Artists are encouraged to experiment with different facial features, hairstyles, and physical characteristics to create unique and captivating portraits.

Simulating texture: Texture adds richness and detail to one-line portraits, particularly in depictions of hair. By varying the stroke style and thickness, artists can simulate different hair textures, enhancing the realism of their artwork.

Adding depth: Adjusting line thickness to create depth and dimensionality is a fundamental technique in realistic one-line art. By making certain lines thicker and others thinner, artists can create the illusion of depth, bringing their portraits to life.

Planning your drawing: Effective planning is essential for creating realistic one-line portraits. Artists should consider expressions, physical traits, texture, and depth during the guideline sketching phase, allowing for a smoother execution of their artwork.

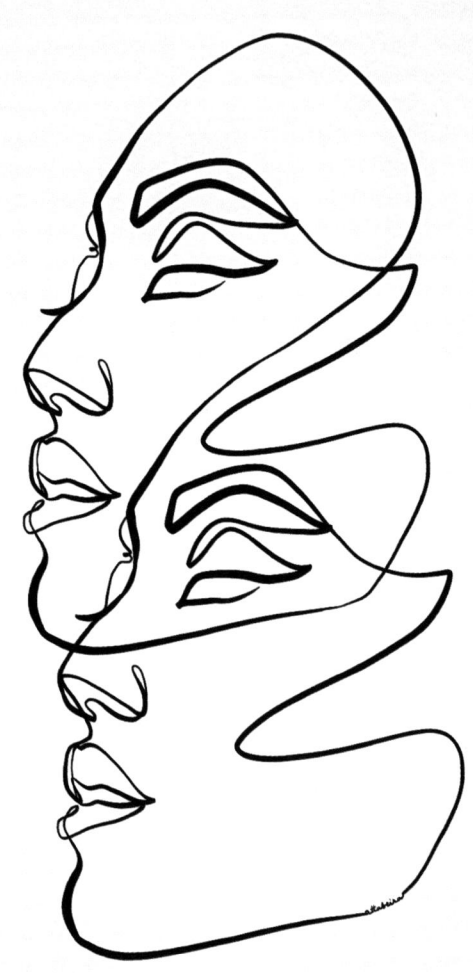

4

Realistic One-Line Art Without Guides

THE PERFORMATIVE ASPECT OF ONE-LINE ART

THERE EXISTS A branch of one-line art that is purely performative. Numerous one-line artists concentrate on refining their stroke stamina, aiming to impress the audience watching them draw. For these artists, part of their craft lies in the ability to produce stunning one-line art without relying on guidelines or reference points. To many, creating one-line art involves imagining what is not on paper and manifesting it into a stroke with a single uninterrupted line.

When it comes to creating realistic one-line art without guidelines, the focus shifts from just the result to the process used to achieve it. In this approach, all the steps of careful planning we discussed earlier happen simultaneously, and some of those steps, like sketching guidelines, occur mentally rather than on paper. This method involves visualizing the subject and its details in the mind's eye while executing each stroke with precision and intention.

Drawing without guidelines is achievable, but it presents particular challenges due to the need for consistent practice and honing of skills. It demands training muscle memory, spatial awareness, and a strong affinity for repetition. Mastering this skill requires dedication and perseverance to develop the ability to visualize and execute precise lines without the aid of reference points.

Achieving Muscle Memory

In the initial chapter of this book, we engaged in some basic muscle memory exercises to loosen up our drawing hand. Now, the muscle-memory exercises we're about to delve into are specifically tailored to train your hand in human face proportions. The ultimate objective is for your hand muscles to instinctively understand where to go to, pause, and pivot when crafting a one-line realistic portrait. The aim is to enable your hand to replicate perspective and proportions consistently, much like it knows how to write cursive letters perfectly each time.

Spatial Awareness

In a one-line portrait done without guidance, spatial awareness is to the eye what muscle memory is to the hand. Training your eyesight to have special awareness allows you to look at your drawing as it is being created and recognize distances and spatial relationships between parts of the face. This skill allows you to assess and correct in real time any mistakes your muscle memory might make. This skill also helps you play with distances and relationships between the features so you can add physical traits,

expressions, and even texture. Spatial awareness is responsible for your ability to customize what your muscle memory does automatically.

Repeat, Repeat, Repeat!

There is no overstating the importance of repeating a specific drawing pose. When I say repeat, I don't mean creating more variations of one-line art with guidance. What I'm emphasizing is truly doing the exact same thing repeatedly. Doing it 50 or 100 times every day for weeks or months. Consider your guideline sketches as training wheels for riding a bike. The more you ride with them, the more comfortable you become. However, at some point, you must take them off to grow.

There is a middle ground between drawing from guidelines and drawing without guidance at all, and that is tracing. Tracing requires you to use guides that you're unfamiliar with. To some extent, you must plan as you go.

The Importance of Tracing

Tracing is a great strategy for improving your ability to create realistic one-line art pieces, and it is a strategy that is often overlooked. Tracing is a technique commonly used in various art styles, and many artists rely on it as a fundamental skill when learning something new. Tracing enables us to begin at the basic level, allowing us to focus on the artistic aspects while providing support in terms of sharpening your muscle memory and spatial awareness.

Tracing can be approached in various ways. As children, we might have placed a blank sheet of paper over an object or image and traced its outline. Back then, tracing was a common practice, and we often found it easier to draw because of it. However, as we grew older, tracing began to feel like cheating, even though it's simply a tool to aid in learning. Nowadays, there are many devices available to make tracing easier, but regardless of the method used, tracing will be a significant part of your learning process moving forward, offering valuable insights and skills along the way.

Realistic one-line art relies heavily on tracing because it allows our hands to develop muscle memory through repetition. Similar to how we learned to write by practicing the same letters repeatedly and tracing them, our hands become accustomed to drawing with realistic proportions through muscle memory. As you continue to trace, it not only becomes easier, but eventually, you'll find yourself able to draw the subject without any assistance.

With that said, tracing using one-line art isn't necessarily easy. You still need to decide where your line goes in a way that looks pleasing, focus on the details that make your subject stand out, and strive to make it look as close to the subject as possible. After all, it's not an abstract drawing—it's a realistic one.

REALISTIC ONE-LINE: NO GUIDANCE/TRACING EXERCISES

Tracing Over Magazines

One way to find ready-made exercises that help you achieve muscle memory and spatial awareness without jumping into no guidance is by opening old magazines and tracing over any portraits you find. Old newspapers work great for this exercise as

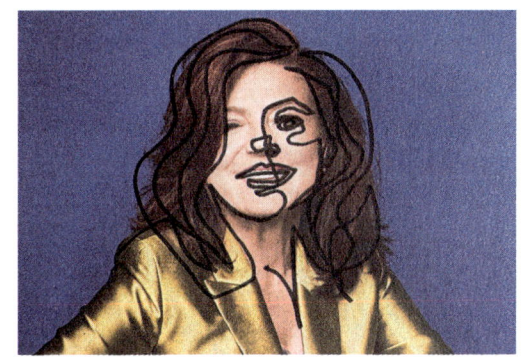

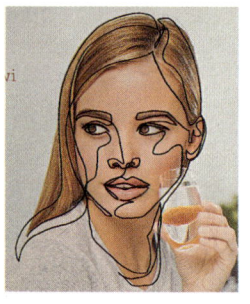 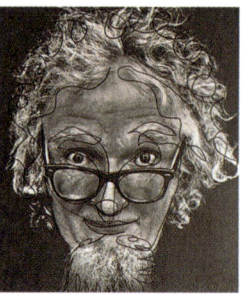

well. I sometimes cut out the portraits and glue them into my sketchbook before tracing over them to keep track of my progress. Above are examples of what mine look like:

Repetition Practice

Print out a photo several times, as many times as possible, and repeat tracing the exact same photo over and over. Pay

attention to the path you choose with your line in each iteration. Decide which iteration you like the most and why. Then, focus on the distances between the facial features of your subject. Observe the details of their nose, lips, eyes, etc., and try to keep your drawings consistent from iteration to iteration.

No-Guidance Test

Looking at your repetition sheets, try to redraw the same subject you've been repeating, but this time without the guidance photo below. Repeat this process several times, aiming to keep the drawing as similar as possible with every iteration.

MY GO-TO LINE STRATEGIES

From Signature Lines to Known Strokes

Another way to ensure that you can create one-line art that does not rely on references or guidance is by recognizing what movements and lines feel comfortable to your hand. These are movements or lines that come up often in the way you draw and kind of feel safe to draw when you're unsure about where to take your line next. These lines or movements tend to work in

just about any drawing and they help you focus more on the feeling and style of the drawing as opposed to focusing on its execution. Your energy goes toward deciding what you want the viewer to feel when they see your work, instead of figuring out how to make the drawing.

These go-to movements are often associated with your personal one-line art style and come from muscle memory and spatial awareness built by repeating your own artistic preferences. They usually take some time to develop, but if you pay close attention, you'll start to see them even when you're just starting out as a one-line artist.

This is why I'm going to share with you my personal go-tos in the hope that they may also work for you. These are moves and strokes I swear by, ones that I can count on to do the job they're intended to do while I'm figuring out all the new things a new drawing throws at me.

Drawing Women

My one-line art style focuses on drawing women. I find that drawing women comes easy to me; I find them simply inspiring. Whenever I draw women, however, there is a lot to pay attention to. The hair often requires me to plan my line path carefully so as to make the drawing look good. There is often too much to think about.

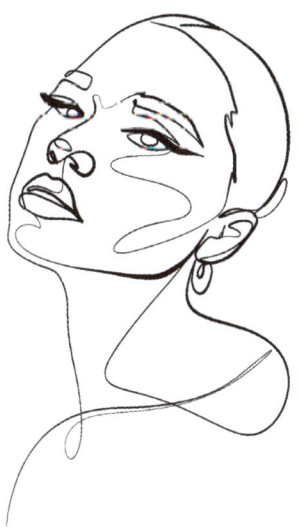

So, when it comes to drawing eyes, I always opt for making the top stroke of the eye thicker and slightly curved in a way so it gives the illusion of the subject wearing makeup. I do this regardless of whether my subject has makeup or not. The line is often not dramatically thicker than the rest of my lines. It is simply a foolproof way for my subject to be considered a woman right off the bat. In the drawing below, I did the same drawing with and without my added "eyeliner" line.

Drawing Men

When it comes to drawing men, I take a different approach. While some men may indeed have long eyelashes, depicting them accurately can sometimes lead the drawing to resemble a woman with short hair. To avoid this, I simplify the eyes and use as few strokes as possible around them. This technique helps create the illusion of a male portrait rather than a female one.

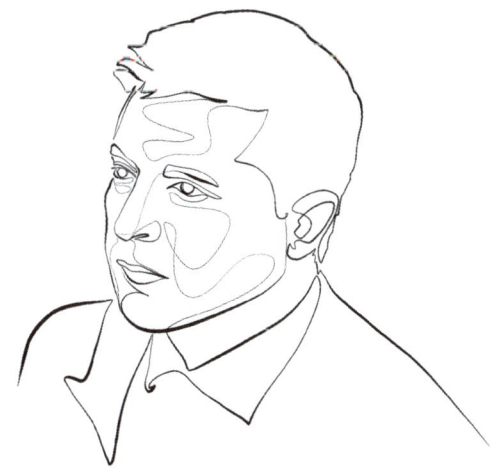

Face-Shadow Permissions

There are occasions when I need to draw a line across the face to continue my one-line drawing on the other side. These interruptions in the flow of the drawing can sometimes make it appear awkward. Through years of experience in one-line art, I've discovered strategic paths around the face using lines that resemble shadows or highlights falling on the face's contours. I typically place these shadow lines on the cheeks or the nose. Here is an example:

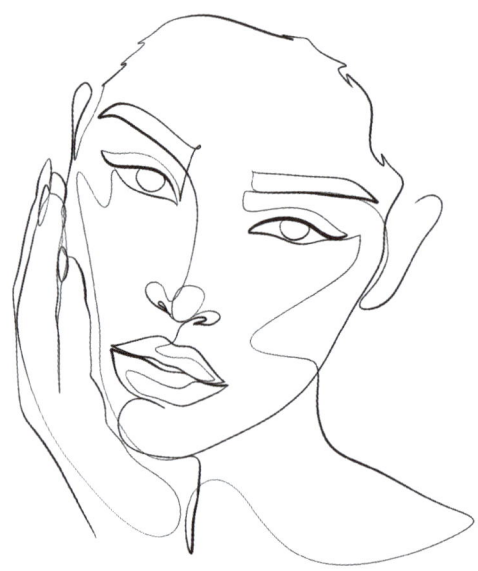

Drawing Noses

Noses can be challenging to capture in one-line art. Initially, I struggled with making the nostrils look natural or realistic. However, I discovered a method that simplifies the process by breaking down the base of the nose into three circular loop movements, representing the two nostrils and the ball of the nose together. Once I adopted this approach, drawing noses in various positions became much easier. Here's a visual representation of what I mean:

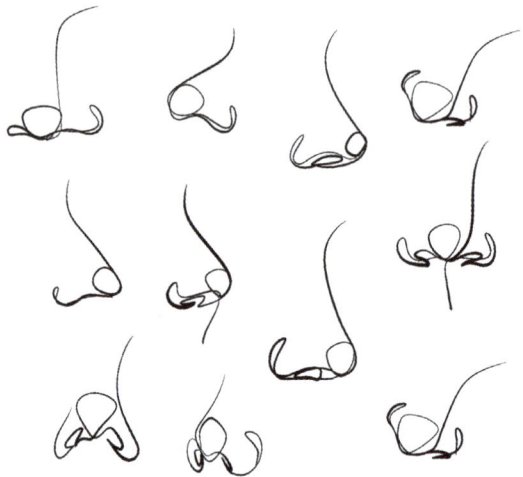

Drawing Toothy Smiles

I found that lines could get out of control when drawing open smiles that show teeth. The number of lines needed for a smile tend to be difficult to portray without it looking crowded. One way to depict a smile with teeth showing is by drawing the rows of teeth with only two lines: one at the top and one at the bottom. The key is to use the line shape to bounce to make it look like each bounce is one individual tooth. I've made an example below.

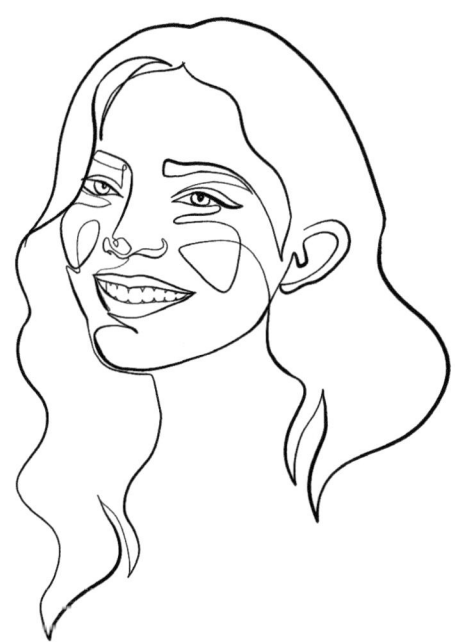

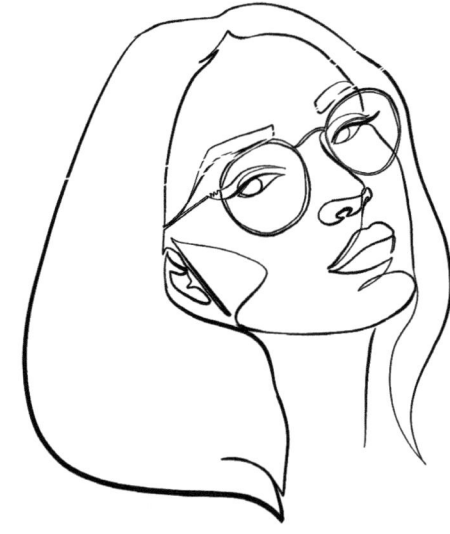

Drawing Beards

Drawing men with thick facial hair presents a challenge similar to drawing glasses. For many individuals, a beard is a defining feature of their appearance and must be accurately depicted. However, beards can occupy a significant portion of

Drawing People Wearing Glasses

Drawing glasses consistently is one of my tried-and-true techniques. However, glasses can pose a challenge because they disrupt the natural flow of facial lines and occupy significant space on the face. Yet, for many people, glasses are an integral part of their appearance, and omitting them would detract from their likeness. When drawing glasses in one-line art, it's crucial to start the line from the eyebrows and connect it to the ears. Typically, the outer and inner rims of the glasses align with the eyebrows, while the sides connect to the upper part of the ears. This approach ensures that the glasses look natural and are seamlessly integrated with the rest of the face.

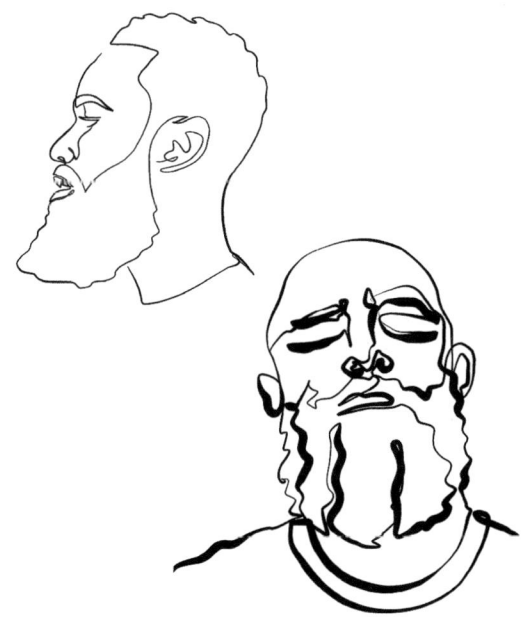

the face, potentially disrupting the overall composition. To address this, it's essential to integrate the beard into the jawline and seamlessly connect it to the hairline. This technique ensures that the beard appears natural and harmoniously blends with the rest of the facial features. In the examples provided on the previous page, observe how the beard in the guy with hair is connected to the hairline, while the beard on the guy with a bald head blends onto his sideburns, maintaining the balance and integrity of the overall portrayal.

Known Paths

One challenge I encountered in my one-line art journey was dealing with disruptive lines cutting across the face from the ear to the mouth. It took me a while to find a solution, but eventually, I discovered a path that has become my go-to approach. Now, when drawing, I always opt for a vertical path to reach the lips, whether starting from the nose or the

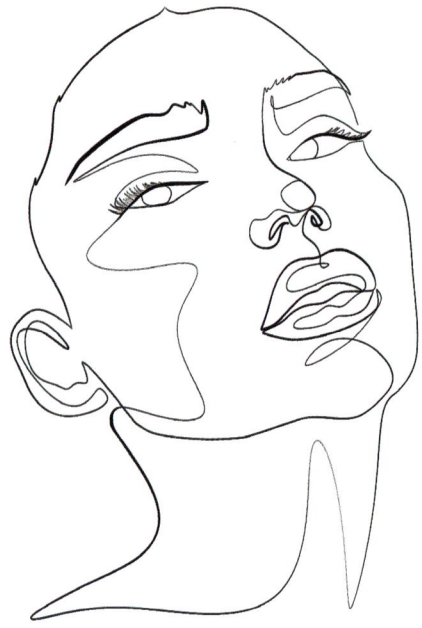

chin. The latter, drawing from the chin, has become particularly common in my work. This technique has become so ingrained in my style that I can often tell if someone has taken my online classes just by observing how they use the chin path in their one-line faces. Here's how it looks:

GO-TO STRATEGIES EXERCISES

EXERCISE 21

Your Go-To Line Strategy

Draw a one-line portrait from memory. Try using at least one of the go-to strategies I've shared with you in this section of the book. Check to see if there are any similar lines between it and the ones you've done so far in this chapter. Are there any lines you keep repeating? Any ways of reaching a facial feature that just feels good to draw for you?

CHAPTER RECAP

Performative aspect: Realistic one-line art without guides is a performative skill, requiring artists to impress audiences with their stroke stamina and ability to visualize and execute precise lines without reference points.

Challenges and skills: Drawing without guides demands consistent practice to develop muscle memory, spatial awareness, and an affinity for repetition. Artists train their hand muscles to instinctively understand proportions and perspectives, while also honing their ability to assess and correct mistakes in real time.

Importance of tracing: Tracing serves as a valuable tool for honing muscle memory and spatial awareness, allowing artists to focus on the artistic aspects of their work while providing support in mastering realistic proportions and details.

Safe, go-to line strategies: Recognizing comfortable movements and lines helps in drawing without references. Personal go-to movements develop from repetition and spatial awareness.

Drawing women: The use of slightly thicker top strokes for eyes to imply makeup, enhancing the femininity of the subject.

Drawing men: Simplify the depiction of male eyes to distinguish male portraits from female ones.

Face-shadow permissions: Strategic placement of lines mimics natural shadows and contours on the face.

Drawing noses: A simplified approach to drawing noses uses three circular loop movements.

Drawing smiles: Depict open smiles with teeth using minimal lines to avoid overcrowding.

Go-to strategies exercises: These exercises encourage experimentation with the author's go-to strategies in one-line portraits drawn from memory, urging artists to identify and develop their own preferred techniques and strokes.

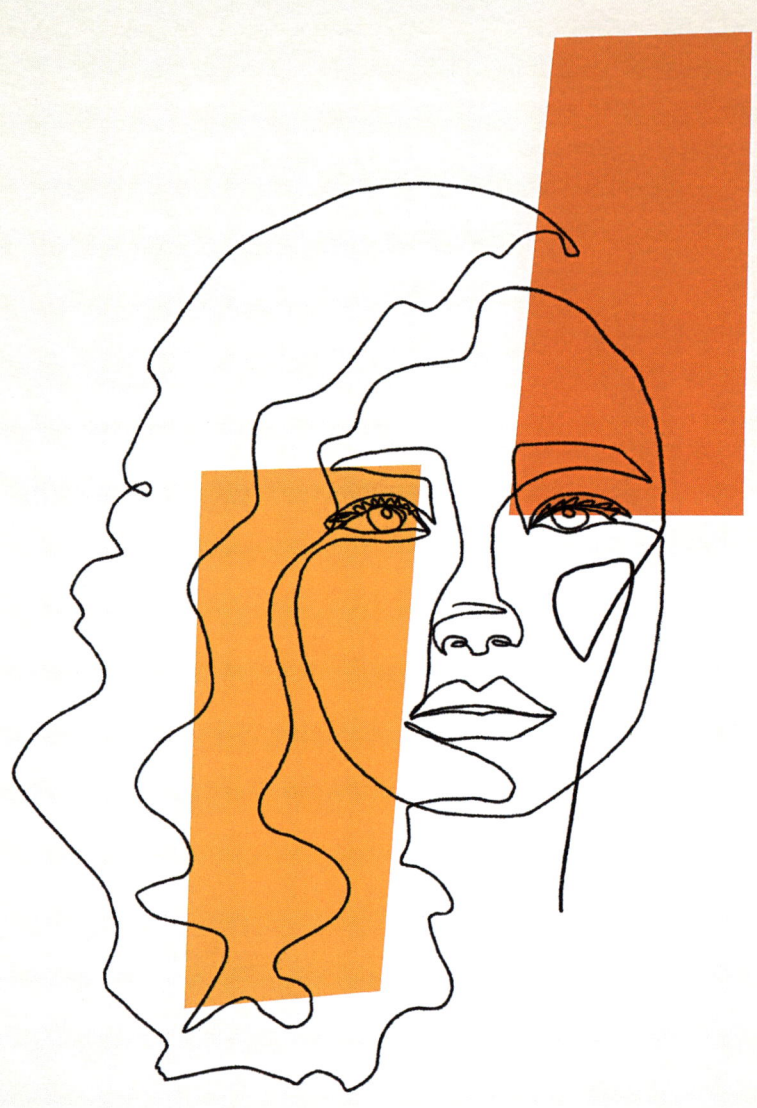

5

Digital One-Line Art

Engaging in digital one-line art is as thrilling as its traditional counterpart, with the convenience of having all necessary tools readily available. This includes not only drawing brushes and line-work tools but also encompasses the practice involved in your one-line art journey.

For digital one-line art we will be using the app Procreate. This app, only available on iPad, has changed the way one-line art can be learned and practiced.

All tools needed for stroke stamina, muscle memory, and spatial awareness are within this application. You can take your iPad with you anywhere and bring your practice with you.

PROCREATE LAYERS

IN PROCREATE, YOU can work with layers, allowing you to have a guidelines layer or an image layer at the bottom while drawing your lines on a top layer, akin to using a pen on a pencil sketch. However, in Procreate, you can easily hide your bottom layer, resulting in drawings that appear as if they were created without any guiding marks in the first place.

This allows people to produce a result similar to those who already have muscle memory and spatial awareness. Procreate became the tool that helps one-line art students reach strong results in a short amount of time.

Adding Color in One-Line Art

While the essence of one-line art lies in its simplicity and the fluid continuity of a single stroke, the strategic addition of color can breathe life into these minimalist creations, adding layers of emotion, depth, and vibrancy. This section explores how artists can thoughtfully incorporate color into their one-line drawings using Procreate, transforming black-and-white simplicity into colorful masterpieces.

Choosing Your Color Palette

Selecting a color palette is the first step in bringing a splash of vibrancy to your one-line art. Consider the emotion or mood you wish to convey with your artwork. Warm colors can evoke feelings of passion and energy, while cool colors can impart calmness and serenity. Procreate's color wheel and palette library allow you to experiment with and save your favorite combinations for easy access.

Tips for choosing colors:

* Use complementary colors for contrast and emphasis.

* Try analogous colors for a harmonious and cohesive look.

* Experiment with monochromatic shades for a subtle and sophisticated vibe.

Procreate has a very cool way to strip color from images. This feature allows you to insert an image on Procreate and ask it to give you a color palette based on the colors that are present in the image. This tool is great for people who love drawing inspiration from the colors in the world around us. From a bird, the sunset, or a flower. Check the QR code below to see how this is done.

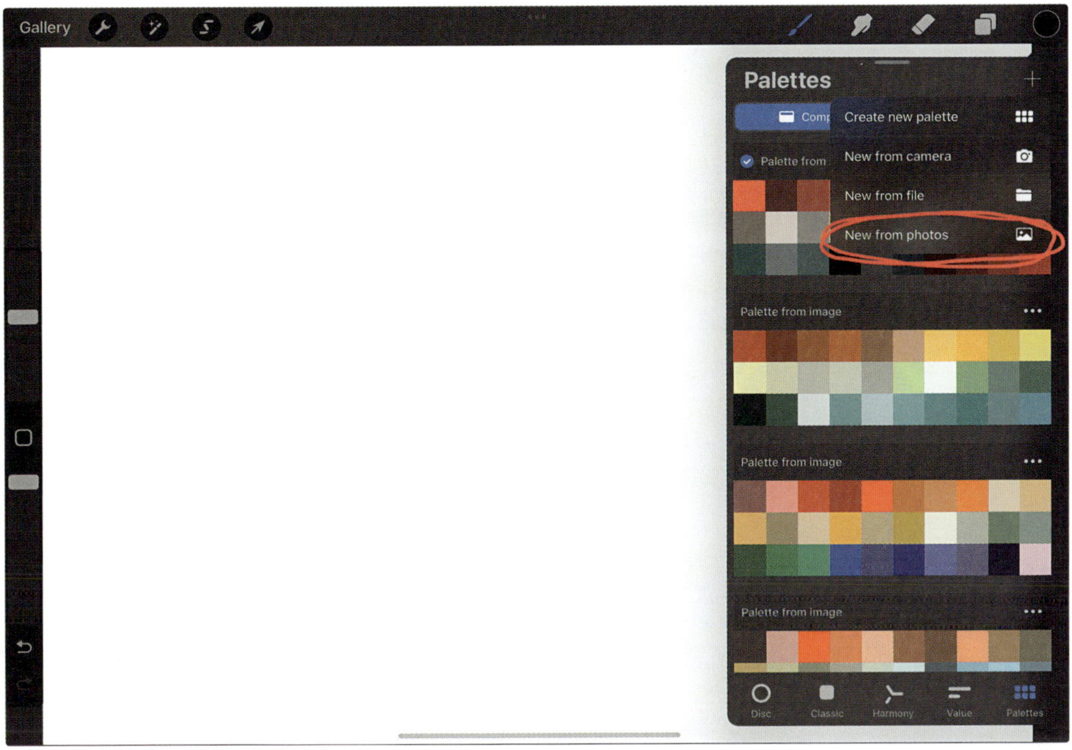

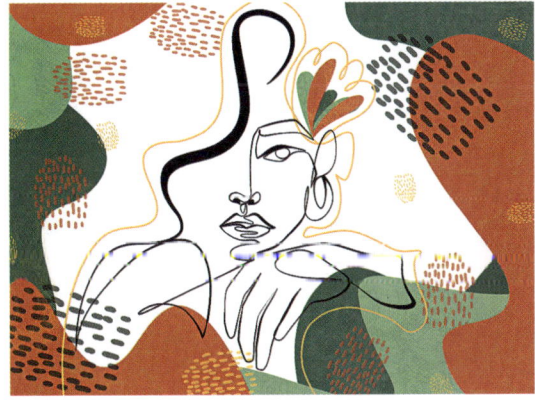

Adding Color Without Breaking the Line

The challenge in one-line art is to integrate color without disrupting the integrity of the single line. Here are two ways to achieve this:

Layering: Use Procreate's layers to apply color beneath your line art. This technique allows you to color freely without modifying the original line. Adjust the layer opacity for a softer effect.

Solid brush strokes: Create shapes and lines that complement your one-line art piece without drawing on top of it. Following the movement of your line in segments always looks pleasing.

COLOR EXERCISES

Colorful Emotions

Create a series of one-line portraits that express different emotions using color. Choose a simple palette for each emotion and experiment with the techniques mentioned above to integrate color into your drawings. Reflect on how color choices impact the overall feel of each piece.

PROCREATE BRUSHES

Ready-Made Brushes

The app Procreate comes with hundreds of awesome brushes for different purposes. These brushes are so close to reality that it is a true joy to use them for the art we create. Since getting the app in 2018, there are three of these brushes I just can't get enough of. These three brushes are my go-to whenever I am not feeling particularly creative or have to tackle a drawing that is proving to be a little more difficult to achieve than others.

In general, these brushes are well-suited for one-line art as they are. This means you can simply select them and start drawing. I'll guide you through how I use each of these three brushes and offer tips on using them effectively. While they work well as they are, I'll also highlight some quirks I've encountered with extended use, which you may find helpful to adjust to over time.

Dry Ink

The first brush I want to show you is the "Dry Ink" brush. You can find it by looking into the Inking brush set. I love the rough feeling this brush gives me. It's great when I want my drawing to look less polished or I am drawing something that is meant to be rough, like a one-line of a statue. I also like it because it looks like chalk or a blunt pencil.

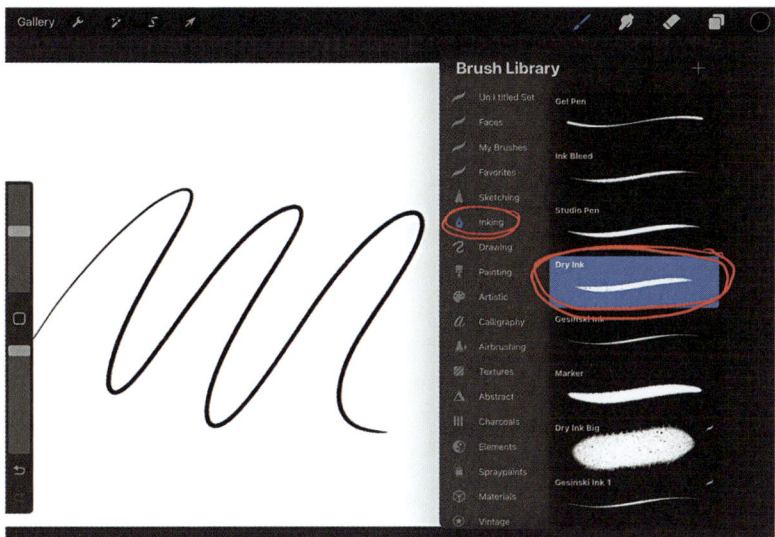

Monoline

I use Monoline every time I need something to look very put together. It is a brush that stays the same width and opacity regardless of how much pressure you put into the iPad screen. I think it is a great brush for getting started with one-line drawing because it is not too sensitive, and it gives a polished, clean result. You can find it by going to the Calligraphy brush set and then tapping on Monoline.

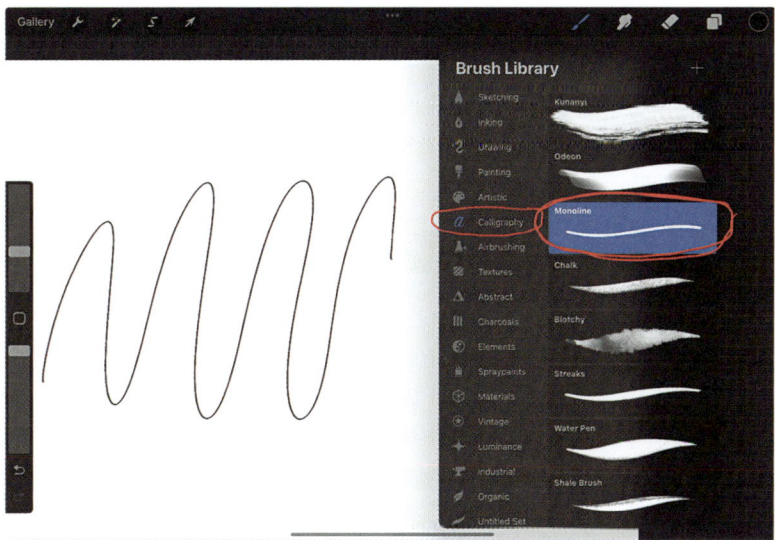

Syrup

This brush is hands down my favorite—it's my artistic soulmate. In fact, I'm so enamored with it that I've already committed to it. Nowadays, there isn't a one-line drawing I attempt without first using the Syrup brush. But like any great love story, mastering this brush wasn't easy. It's incredibly responsive to pressure, and since the iPad screen is glass, it took a lot of practice before I could create my best pieces with it.

The Syrup brush has a striking quality to it. When you apply more pressure, the brush stroke widens quickly, creating a thick line. Conversely, with a lighter touch, the line can be as thin as a hair strand. I absolutely adore its versatility.

To locate it, simply navigate to the Inking brush set, and you'll find Syrup waiting for you there.

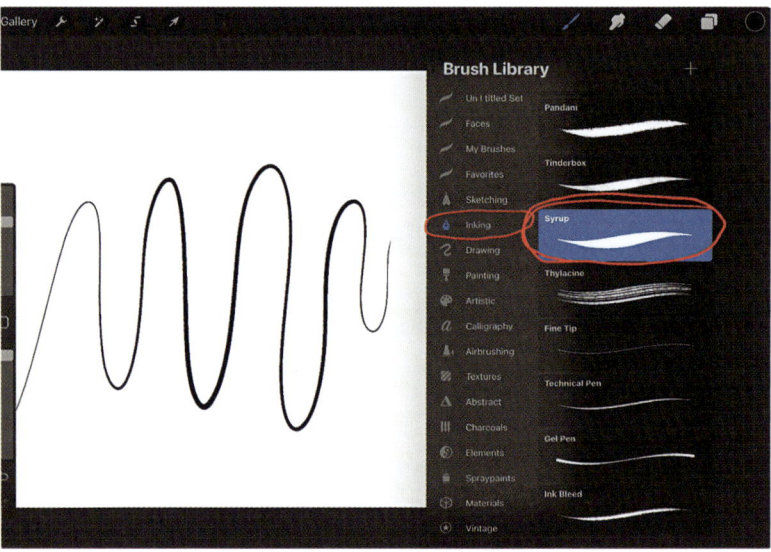

The Art of One-Line Drawing

A Way to Personalize the Brushes You Use

Brush studio is Procreate's section for altering, personalizing, and creating brushes for the app. The app gives you free rein in there so that you can personalize their default brushes, like the ones we just went over, or even create your own brushes from scratch. Enter the Brush Studio by tapping twice in any of the Procreate brushes.

There are three main areas in the Brush studio interface: The first one is the leftmost column that has all the brush attributes. For one-line art, the attributes I work with most frequently are stabilization, tapper, and properties. The second column is properties, the amounts you can alter within those attributes. Here is where you'll do the actual changing. The third and widest column is a drawing pad for testing.

Quick erasing tip: In the drawing pad, just motion side to side with three fingers on the screen.

Whenever a brush does not suit me perfectly, there are three attributes I always look into, and tweaking them a little usually solves the issue causing that particular brush to feel a little off. Here are my go-to attributes to tweak and what they do:

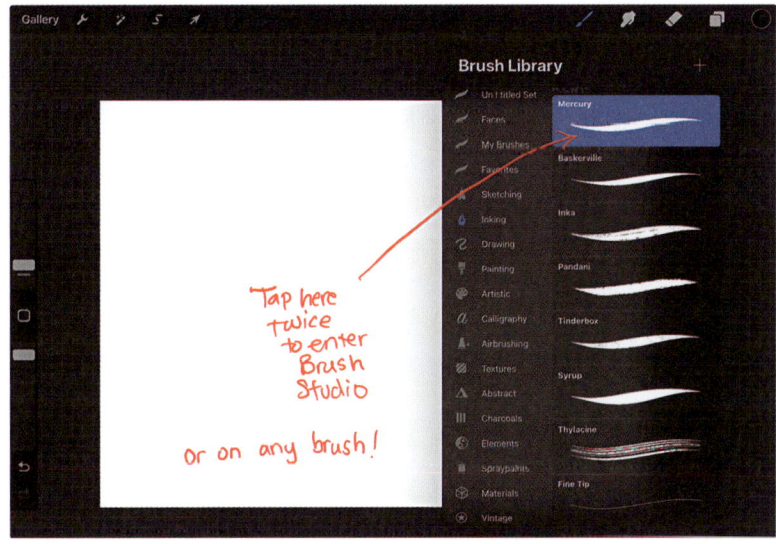

Tap here twice to enter Brush Studio

or on any brush!

Stabilization and StreamLine

After years and years of practice I use it less and less. But it was definitely a game changer for me when my stroke was not as stable as it is now. This attribute is ideal for people whose line looks very shaky. Stabilization smooths out strokes as you draw them. This makes hand-drawn lines straighter than they would naturally be and StreamLine assists in smoothing out any wobbles or shakes in your line. StreamLine is particularly important for inking and calligraphy.

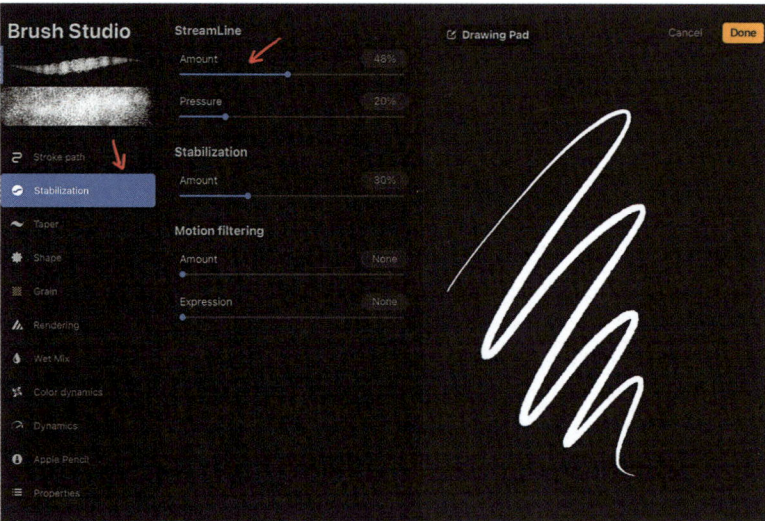

Tapper

I use this one when I want a brush's pattern, but the points are very blunt and not suited for my one-line art style. This attribute helps turn any Procreate brush with a pattern you like into a more one-line-art-friendly brush. Tapper adjusts your brushes thickness and opacity at the beginning and end of your stroke. It helps give your brush a natural, tapered appearance at the beginning or at the end of your stroke.

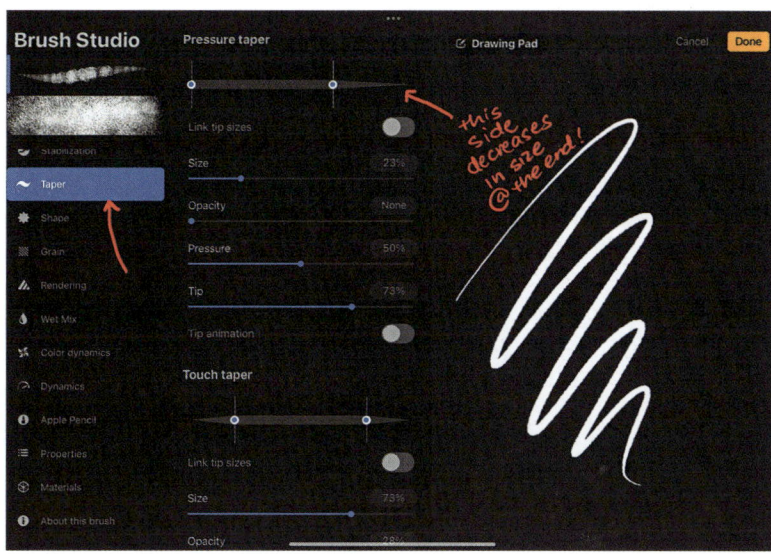

Properties: Brush Behavior

If you haven't already noticed, I'm on a mission to make every brush behave like my beloved Syrup. One of the final adjustments I typically make is to customize the brush behavior. Within the properties, the Brush behavior section sets boundaries for size and opacity. These settings determine the maximum and minimum limits of the size and opacity sliders in the Procreate sidebar.

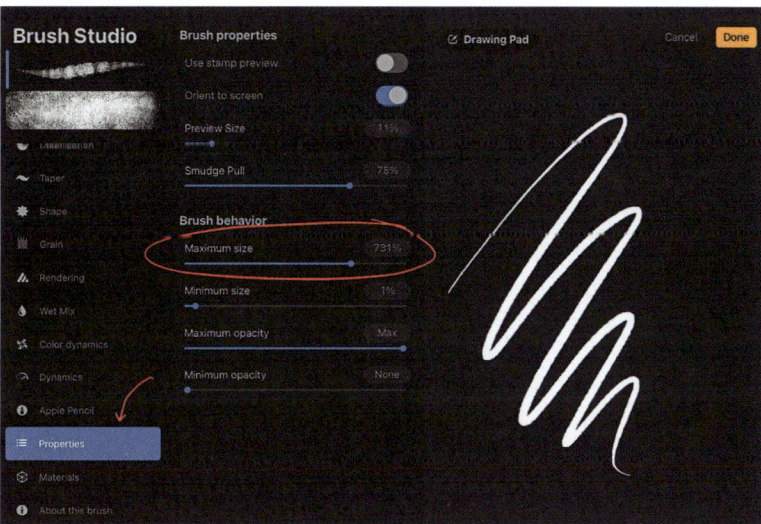

PERSONALIZED ONE-LINE ART BRUSHES

Perfected Over the Years

I have worked on the three brushes I mentioned before for years and have perfected these brushes specifically for one-line art use. You are welcome to use them as well, since they've already been altered and you won't have to put your practice on pause to set up the ones that come with the app. You can also edit my brushes to accommodate your specific needs, but at least you will be able to hit the ground running. To download my one-line brushes, scan the QR code below and follow the instructions to bring them into procreate.

Importing a Brush File Into Procreate

Whether you've created your own brush, found a perfect one online, or are simply using the ones I've gifted to you above, importing it into Procreate can unlock new dimensions in your digital art. Follow these simple steps to add new brushes to your Procreate brush library.

Step 1: Download the brush file

First, ensure the brush file (.brush or .brushset) is downloaded to your iPad. This might involve downloading it from a website, email, or cloud storage service. If you're downloading the file directly on your iPad, it will likely go to your Downloads folder within the Files app.

Step 2: Locate the file

Open the Files app on your iPad and navigate to the location of the downloaded brush file. If you're not sure where it was saved, try looking in the Downloads folder under the "On My iPad" section.

Step 3: Share to Procreate

Tap and hold on the brush file, then select the Share option from the pop-up menu. In the Share Sheet that appears, scroll through the apps until you find Procreate, then tap on it. Procreate will open automatically.

Step 4: Importing the brush

Once Procreate opens, the brush or brush set will automatically import to your brush library. If you've imported a single brush, Procreate will place it in the "Imported" brush set. If you've imported a brush set, you'll find a new brush set with the name of the file you imported in your brush library.

Alternative Method: Importing From Procreate

If you prefer to import directly from within Procreate, follow these steps:

Open Procreate and tap on the brush icon to open the Brush Library.

Swipe down until you see the "+" icon at the top-right corner of the Brush Library. Tap on it to create a new brush set (if you're importing a single brush and want to keep your library organized).

With your new brush set selected, tap the "+" button at the top-right corner of the library to bring up the brush-creation menu. Here, choose "Import" at the top right.

Navigate through the Files app interface that appears to find and select your downloaded brush or brush-set file. Once selected, it will import directly into the brush set you've created or the current selection.

Importing an Image Into Procreate for Tracing

Tracing over images can be an invaluable practice method, helping to refine your

skills in proportions, perspective, and detailing. Procreate simplifies this process by allowing you to import images directly into your canvas and trace over them using layers. Here's how you can bring an image into Procreate and set yourself up for tracing:

Step 1: **Open Procreate and select your canvas**
Start by opening the Procreate app on your iPad. From the "Gallery" view, either create a new canvas by tapping the "+" icon in the top-right corner or open an existing project where you wish to import the image.

Step 2: **Accessing the Actions menu**
With your canvas open, look to the top-left corner of the screen to find the wrench icon, which opens the Actions menu. Tap on it to reveal a variety of options.

Step 3: **Importing the image**
In the Actions menu, select the "Add" tab to find various options for adding content to your canvas. Tap on "Insert a photo." This will bring up your iPad's photo library. Navigate through your albums to find the image you want to trace. Once you find the image, tap on it to select, and it will be automatically imported into your canvas.

Step 4: Adjusting the imported image

After your image is imported, it will appear on a new layer in your canvas. You can use Procreate's transformation tool (the arrow icon in the top menu) to adjust the size, rotation, and position of the image to fit your needs. Pinch with two fingers to resize or rotate, and then drag to move the image. Tap the "arrow" icon again to confirm your adjustments.

Step 5: Preparing to trace

Once your image is positioned correctly, it's time to prepare for tracing. Tap the layers icon (two overlapping squares) in the top-right corner to open the Layers Panel. You'll see your image on its own layer. Tap the "N" on the layer to adjust the opacity, sliding left to make the image lighter. This makes it easier to see your tracing lines over the top.

Step 6: Creating a new layer for tracing

With the Layers Panel still open, tap the "+" icon at the top of the panel to create a new layer above your imported image. This layer is where you will do your tracing, keeping it separate from the original image layer.

Step 7: Start tracing

Select the new layer you just created for tracing. Choose your preferred brush and color, then start tracing over the image. The lightened image beneath will guide you as you draw on the layer above.

Step 8: Hiding the original image

After you've finished tracing, you can hide the original image layer to view your tracing by itself. In the Layers Panel, uncheck the checkbox next to the image layer you imported. This will leave only your tracing visible on the canvas.

Tips for Successful Tracing

* Use a variety of brushes for different effects and line weights in your tracing.

* Zoom in for detailed sections to ensure accuracy.

* Practice with different images to enhance your understanding of form and structure.

More Than Procreate

Exploring digital art tools beyond Procreate opens a world of possibilities. And though it is true that most one-line artists opt for Procreate, each software has something unique to offer, with each of them fitting different styles and needs. Let's check out a few:

Adobe Fresco: This app is great for artists who love the feel of painting and drawing by hand. Fresco's live brushes mimic real paint and ink, making digital art feel more natural. It's perfect if you're already using Adobe products and want something that syncs up easily with tools like Photoshop.

Autodesk Sketchbook: This one's all about simplicity. If you want a clean, straightforward app that lets you focus on drawing without getting bogged down in menus, Sketchbook is a solid choice. It's user-friendly, making it ideal for beginners and pros alike who just want to get their ideas down.

Adobe Illustrator: If you're into vector art or looking for crisp, clean lines that you can scale up or down without losing quality, Adobe Illustrator is worth a look. This one is perfect if you're already using Adobe products and want something that syncs up easily with tools like Adobe Creative Cloud.

Picking the Right Tool

Choosing the right software isn't just about which one has the coolest features; it's about what fits your workflow and style. Like trying on shoes, you want something that feels comfortable and suits your needs. Most of these tools offer free trials, so give them a spin. See which one clicks with you and your way of making art.

Remember, the best tool is the one that you enjoy using and that helps you bring your creative vision to life.

PROCREATE EXERCISES

EXERCISE 22

One-Line Drawing of a Woman

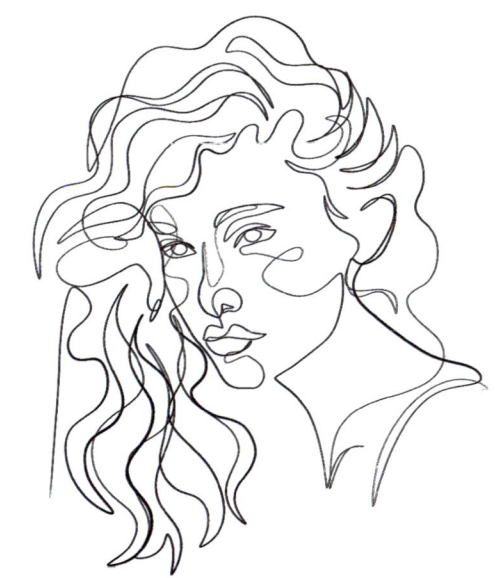

Using the tracing method on Procreate, choose the photo of a woman to use as reference for one-line art. Take into account the different skills we worked on in chapters 3 and 4. When done tracing, toggle the visibility of your reference image to look at your final drawing.

One-Line Drawing of a Man

Once again using the tracing method on Procreate, choose the photo of a man to use as reference for one-line art. Try using a different Procreate brush for this one. Take into account the different skills we worked on in chapters 3 and 4. When done tracing, toggle the visibility of your reference image to look at your final drawing.

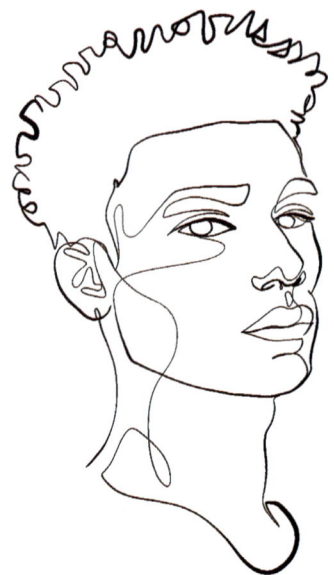

CHAPTER RECAP

Introduction to Procreate: Procreate, available only on iPad, revolutionizes digital one-line art by providing all necessary tools for stroke stamina, muscle memory, and spatial awareness conveniently in one application.

Procreate Layers: Working with layers in Procreate allows artists to have a guiding layer or image layer at the bottom while drawing lines on top. Hiding the bottom layer results in drawings appearing as if they were created without guiding marks.

Adding color in one-line art: This section explores the strategic addition of color to one-line drawings in Procreate, emphasizing how color can enhance the emotional depth and visual appeal of minimalist art. It provides tips on selecting color palettes and integrating color without compromising the unity of the line.

Procreate brushes:

Dry Ink: This brush is ideal for creating rough-looking drawings like statues, resembling chalk or a blunt pencil.

Monoline: This brush maintains consistent width and opacity regardless of pressure, offering a clean, polished result.

Syrup: This is a highly versatile brush with pressure responsiveness, allowing thick or thin lines depending on pressure applied.

Brush Studio: The studio allows you to personalize and create brushes within Procreate, offering attributes like stabilization, taper, and properties for customization.

Importing images and tracing: Procreate simplifies importing images for tracing, enabling artists to use reference photos as layers and toggle their visibility for tracing.

Exploring beyond Procreate: This section briefly reviews other digital art tools like Adobe Fresco, Autodesk Sketchbook, and Adobe Illustrator, suggesting that artists experiment with different software to find the best fit for their style and workflow.

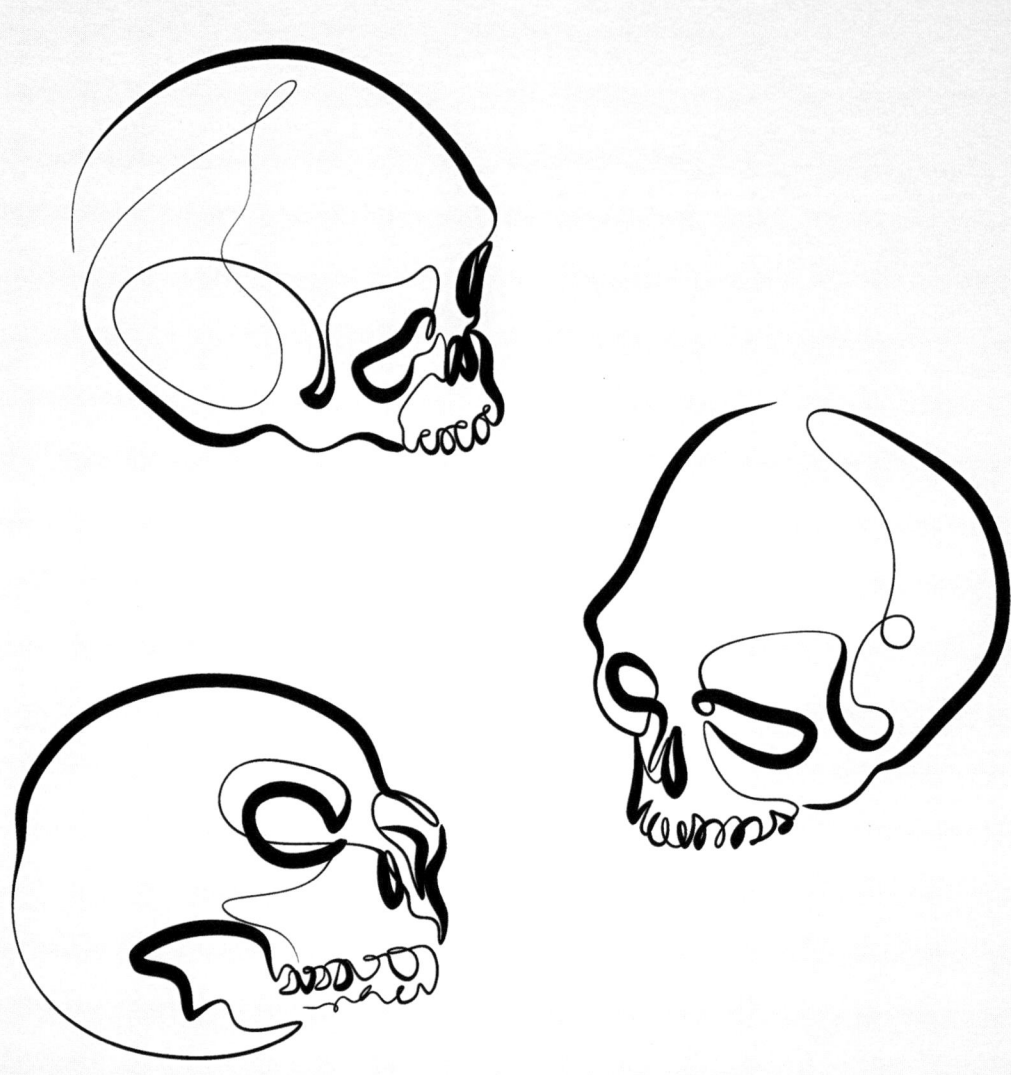

6

Common One-Line Art Mistakes

With more than 10,000 one-line art students, it is only natural to find that a lot of these students make similar mistakes. These mistakes have simple solutions, so I thought it was important to dedicate a whole chapter to addressing the fact that they do exist and how to best solve them. These are common mistakes, and one cannot really avoid them. They're a byproduct of the learning processes we have discussed in this book so far.

You may also encounter issues specific to your unique one-line style. In such cases, this book may not provide solutions. When facing challenges related to your one-line style, you'll need to rely on practice and repetition to find solutions on your own. The more you encounter a particular mistake, the better you'll become at resolving it.

Troubleshooting Your Own Work

Reflecting on your own artwork and troubleshooting when you encounter challenges can be daunting if you're unsure how to find solutions independently. In such situations, studying the work of other artists can be immensely helpful. By observing the diverse approaches of different one-line artists, you'll gain insights into various solutions for common problems.

So, whenever you're uncertain about how to address a problem not covered here, don't hesitate to turn to the internet. Explore the work of other one-line artists to see how they tackle similar challenges in their art.

PROBLEM 1

Lines Crossing the Face

Problem: Your one-line face has lines across the cheek. You feel you have to connect the mouth to the rest of the face, but you don't like how it looks when the piece is finalized.

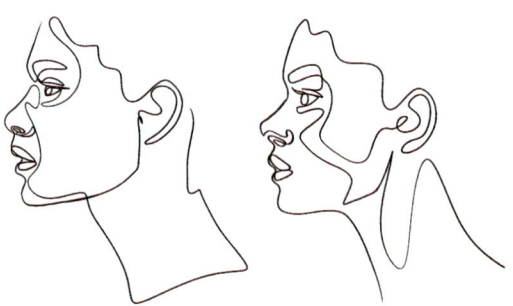

Solution: In one-line portraits, not all lines are the same. When drawing the perimeter of the face, it's important to reserve horizontal lines for depicting beards and mustaches only. If your subject doesn't have a mustache or beard, aim to create most, if not all, lines from top to bottom. This helps avoid giving the impression of slicing across the face.

PROBLEM 2

Lines Without a Purpose

Problem: The lines you make are simply there to connect one part of the face to the other. They make your drawing look messy and with lines that are not needed. You feel like you're tracing over the same features over and over.

Solution: The solution to this problem is not very obvious because instead of one simple solution, it has a two-part, compound way to solve the problem. Every single line in your drawing should have a clear purpose. By this I mean that it should be depicting something within the subject. A line made simply for the purpose of connecting one part of the face to the other will always stand out and disrupt the visual flow of the piece.

First step: Use the thick-and-thin line approach to make less important "connection" lines less visible. Merge them into the background by making them thinner.

The viewer will notice your important, thicker lines first and will only notice your less important connection lines later.

Second step: Use hidden shadows in facial features to connect your lines through so they go from being connection lines to being shadows and folds lines. They will now have a purpose other than simply connecting between features.

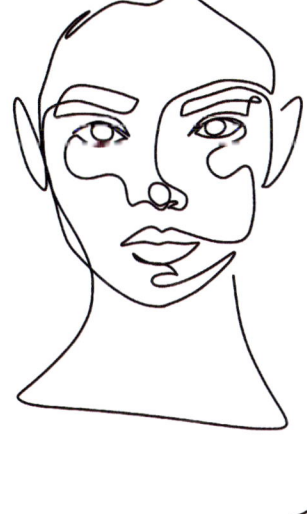

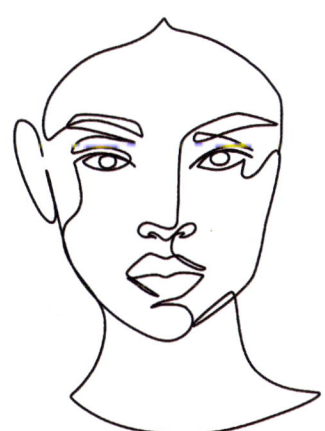

Crowded Lines

Problem: There are sections in your drawing with so many intersecting lines that are crammed together. These lines are coming from different directions but have to pass through similar spaces, making it difficult to know where the line goes after it gets into the clump. This makes it impossible for people to follow the path of your line.

Solution: The solution here is very simple. Take a close look at the zoomed-in drawing under this section. Notice how I carefully avoid crossing my lines at the very same point. The trick is to cross the lines at different moments to avoid the clump. This will allow the viewer to follow the line path with the gaze or finger to check that it is indeed a one-line drawing.

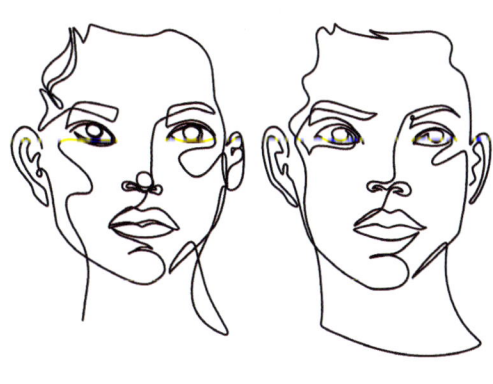

PROBLEM-SOLVING EXERCISES

Solve This Problem

The drawing below has one problem that could use solving. Find what can be improved in the line work in this piece and redraw it with the solution that best fits this particular problem.

Solve This Problem

The drawing below has one problem that could use solving. Find what other parts of your subject can be represented to solve this problem.

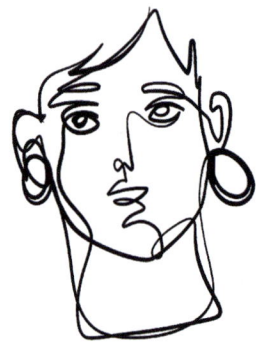

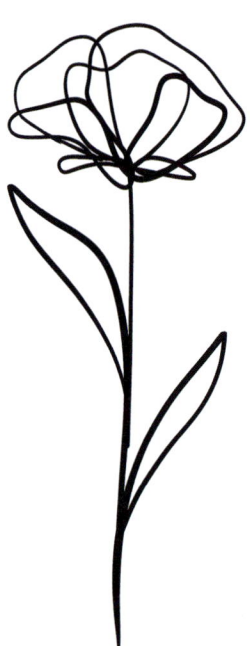

Solve This Problem

The drawing below has one problem that could use solving. What other ways can you make your subject's features more visually appealing?

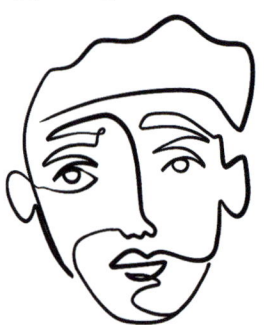

CHAPTER RECAP

Acknowledgment of learning from mistakes: Mistakes are an inevitable and natural part of the learning curve in one-line art, common among both novices and seasoned artists. These mistakes are viewed as opportunities for growth rather than setbacks.

Self-troubleshooting and external inspiration: This section stresses the value of self-reflection and independent problem-solving when encountering stylistic challenges. It also recommends studying the work of various one-line artists as a source of inspiration and solutions for overcoming common obstacles.

The chapter offers insight on how to fix cramped lines, connection lines, and lines disrupting the drawing.

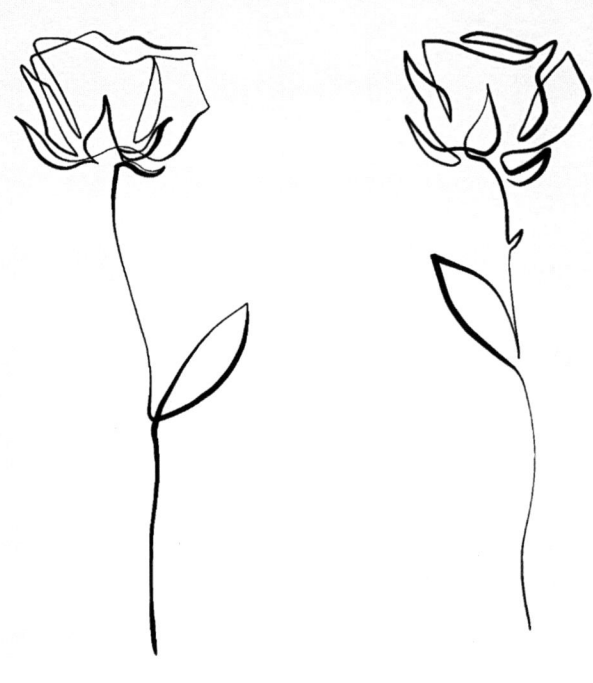

7

One-Line Art Styles

DISCOVERING YOUR PERSONAL ONE-LINE-ART STYLE

EVEN WITHIN THE realm of one-line art, artists employ various approaches to producing their lines. While artists might assume that one-line art, being simple and minimalistic, wouldn't allow for much stylistic variety, it's surprising to discover that the four different styles we'll explore in this chapter represent only a small fraction of the styles I've encountered in the art world.

In this chapter, we'll explore the four most common line styles I've encountered. Each of these styles is a valid approach to one-line art, and I've personally used all of them at various points in my one-line art career. Each style serves a different purpose—one might be suitable for book illustrations, while another might be better suited for a product label.

Being well versed in all these one-line styles will make you a more well-rounded one-line artist. Even if the style is not entirely to your liking, the ability to work in any style gives you more versatility as an artist. The more styles you learn, the more you are able to draw from when crafting your own personal one-line style.

Reproducing Styles Is the Way to Grow

Style analysis and style studies are two of the skills that I work on most frequently with my students. These skills will allow you to look critically at any one-line piece, and then decode the way it was made and the reason it was made the way it was. In addition, these skills will also enable you to reproduce the style you're observing because of your ability to decode it.

Attempting to replicate the work of other artists, exactly as it appears, is beneficial for understanding their skill set and fostering your own artistic growth. I strongly encourage you to incorporate copying into your practice routine and your journey in one-line art, especially after you've finished reading this book.

That said, it's crucial to always credit the artists whose work you're copying. Presenting copied one-line art as your own is never acceptable. Copying for the purpose of growth and practice while acknowledging and crediting the original artists is the proper way to go.

Common One-Line Art Styles

In this section, we'll define and identify the four most common one-line art styles frequently encountered in the one-line art world. It's important to note that these styles may sometimes blend elements from one or more categories. While the examples provided here are clearly delineated, real-world instances may not always neatly fit into one category or another.

I strongly encourage you to continue observing various one-line art styles to enrich and enhance your own work. To highlight the significant differences between these styles, I've created the same exact drawing using each style to demonstrate how they differ from one another. Below are four one-line styles for you to consider:

Amorphous one-line art: The term "Amorphous" means "without form." Amorphous one-line art is characterized by some resemblance to the object being drawn, but the shape can be somewhat distorted. This is one of my favorite styles because it allows for free-flowing drawing without worrying too much about the precise size of each part.

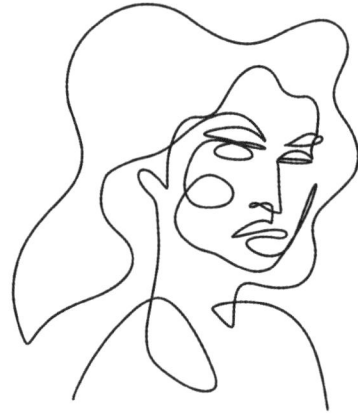

Geometric one-line art: This style uses geometric shapes and sharp turns instead of soft curves to compose the one-line drawing. The style also makes use of perfect geometric shapes such as circles, rectangles, and squares to make the drawing look put together and mechanical as opposed to making it look organic.

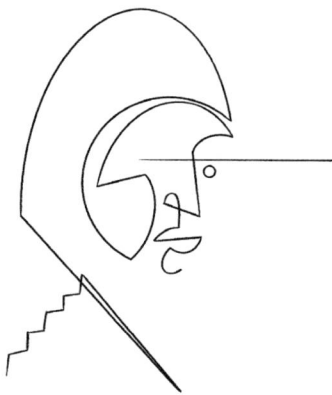

creates an impression of depth because thicker lines appear closer to us compared to thinner ones.

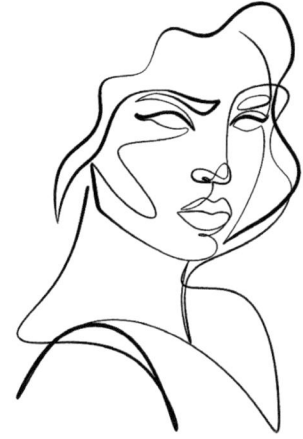

Curved one-line art: This style is known as the curved one-line style. Unlike our previous styles, it consists of curves and freely shaped circles drawn by hand. The use of curves and circles gives this one-line drawing a bubbly and bouncy appearance.

Your One-Line Art Style

This is a good moment to start thinking about what your personal one-line art style could look like. As you continue to practice and take inspiration from various styles, including those mentioned above, as well as the lines that feel most natural to your hand, you'll gradually develop your unique style. Similar to handwriting, your one-line style becomes distinctively yours, serving as a signature element. The specific details you incorporate into your art will become recognizable traits that viewers associate with your work.

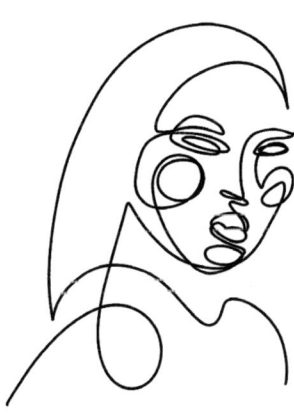

Style Analysis

Analyzing various styles is an invaluable skill for one-line artists. Whenever you come across one-line artwork, take a moment to observe how the artist tackles

Thick and thin one-line art: The thick and thin one-line drawing style is my go-to when creating my own art. It's the style I've adopted as my own, and it's my favorite to use while drawing. This style

common challenges encountered in one-line art. How do they connect facial lines when working on a portrait? How do they prevent clumping to keep their line path clean? And how do they avoid creating lines that serve solely as connections? These observations can provide valuable insights into different approaches and techniques.

Styles Studies

Another essential skill is conducting style studies for yourself. A style study involves practicing a particular style or technique by studying and replicating the work of different artists. I often fill pages in my sketchbook with copies of artwork by various artists, simply to see if I can replicate their style and learn from the process.

Critiquing One-Line Art

When conducting style studies and analyzing different styles, you'll inevitably notice that artists approach things differently than you would. You might observe them making what appears to be a "mistake" or disregarding principles you've learned. However, it's important to keep an open mind because art is subjective. The artist may not be aware of the information you've learned from this book or through your own practice. It's also possible that the artist intentionally deviated from traditional techniques, and what seems like a "mistake" was actually deliberate. Keeping an open mind and being respectful is always the way to take in somebody else's work. Especially if we would like other people to do the same with ours.

ONE-LINE STYLE EXERCISES

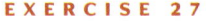

EXERCISE 27

Amorphous One-Line Art

Considering the characteristics of amorphous one-line art, I recommend creating three to five one-line drawings in this style. Repetition is key here, as it allows your hand muscles and spatial awareness to adapt to the style, making it feel more

natural over time. The more you practice, the more comfortable you'll become with this approach to drawing.

EXERCISE 28

Geometric One-Line Art

For this exercise, take some time to explore the geometric one-line art style by creating three to five drawings that embody its characteristics. Replicating this style multiple times is beneficial as it allows you to become more familiar with its principles and techniques. With each drawing, focus on incorporating sharp lines and geometric shapes, maintaining precision and consistency throughout. As you practice, you'll notice your ability to create intricate geometric patterns and designs improving, enhancing your proficiency in this style.

EXERCISE 29

Curved One-Line Art

Now it is time to do the same exercise for the curved one-line art style. Set aside some time to create three to five drawings that embody the fluidity and softness characteristic of this style. Remember, repetition is key to mastering any technique, so aim to create multiple iterations. With each drawing, focus on smoothly transitioning between curves and hand-shaped circles, capturing the playful and bouncy essence of the curved style. As you continue to practice, your muscle memory will gradually adapt, enhancing your ability to create captivating curved one-line artworks.

EXERCISE 30

Thick and Thin One-Line Art

As we dive into this exercise, you might find the thick and thin one-line art style more familiar, as it's frequently demonstrated in my teaching. Now, let's conduct a style study focusing on mastering the variation in line thickness. Aim to create three to five iterations of drawings, but feel free to do more if you're inclined. As you draw, practice applying pressure to achieve thicker lines and lightly lifting your hand for thinner lines. With each iteration, focus on refining your control over line thickness, gradually honing your skills in this versatile style.

CHAPTER RECAP

Exploration of one-line art styles: Each style, from amorphous to geometric, curved, and thick and thin, serves unique artistic purposes, such as book illustrations or product labels, showcasing the versatility and range of one-line art.

Reproducing styles for growth: Replicating the work of other artists is a crucial exercise for understanding different techniques and fostering personal growth, with a reminder to credit original artists when practicing their styles.

Common one-line art styles:

Amorphous one-line art: Characterized by a loose resemblance to the object, this style allows for free-flowing drawing without strict adherence to exact sizes or shapes.

Geometric one-line art: Use geometric shapes, such as perfect circles, rectangles, and squares, as well as sharp turns to create a mechanical and organized appearance.

Curved one-line art: Emphasizing curves and hand-drawn circles, this style gives the artwork a bubbly and dynamic feel.

Thick and thin one-line art: This style favors a mix of line thicknesses to create depth, with thicker lines suggesting closeness and thinner lines indicating distance.

Discovering personal one-line art style:

Artists should draw inspiration from various styles and the natural tendencies of their hand movements to develop a unique one-line style, which becomes as distinctive as their handwriting.

Style analysis and studies: Critically observing and replicating different one-line art styles helps artists to understand their execution and underlying principles. This process aids in developing a comprehensive skill set and the ability to adapt to various artistic challenges.

Critiquing one-line art: Maintaining an open mind when analyzing other artists' work is important because art is subjective. What may initially appear as mistakes could be intentional stylistic choices, underscoring the subjective nature of art and the importance of respectful critique.

Conclusion

THE ART OF ONE-LINE DRAWING

EMBARKING ON THE journey of one-line art is like opening a door to a world where simplicity and complexity dance in harmony. I hope this book has been a guide, a companion, and a catalyst for exploring the boundless possibilities that lie within a single, uninterrupted line.

From the foundational strokes to the more complex techniques that bring depth and life to minimalist sketches, we have covered a lot, but not all, that there is to learn. As we reach the end of this journey, let's weave together the insights and lessons from each chapter, highlighting the essence of community engagement and the indispensable value of perseverance.

The Essence of One-Line Art

Starting points: We began with the basics, the very foundation of one-line art, where we learned to appreciate the power of simplicity. This initial step was about understanding that complexity isn't necessary for beauty or impact. Through exercises and examples, we saw how a single line could capture emotions, landscapes, and life itself.

Skill building: As our journey progressed, we dove into various techniques designed to enhance our skills. From mastering muscle memory to the art of drawing from memory, we tackled challenges that tested our limits and expanded our capabilities. Each chapter served as a milestone, marking our growth and encouraging us to push further.

The digital canvas: Entering the digital realm opened up a new frontier for our one-line art exploration. Tools like Procreate introduced us to an environment where experimentation wasn't just encouraged; it was limitless. Here, mistakes became lessons, and the undo button was a reminder that in art, as in life, second chances are invaluable.

BEYOND THE PAGES

The Power of Community

Art, at its core, is a form of communication—a way to share parts of ourselves with the world. Engaging with the online art community, sharing your work, and seeking feedback transform the solitary act of drawing into a shared experience. Platforms like Instagram, art forums, and digital galleries are not just showcases but classrooms where we learn from each other.

The Role of Persistence

If there's a single thread that runs through every technique, story, and piece of advice in this book, it's the critical importance of persistence. The path to proficiency in one-line art is paved with trials and errors, each teaching us something valuable. Embracing practice with patience and dedication is how we refine our craft and discover our unique voice in the vast world of art.

Expanding Your Horizon

Continual growth: The journey of a one-line artist is perpetual. Every line you draw, every shape you create, is a step toward understanding not just the art form but yourself. Your style will evolve, influenced by experiences, emotions, and the endless inspiration that life offers. Keep seeking, learning, and growing.

Embracing the community: The art community is a rich tapestry of individuals from diverse backgrounds, each with their own stories and insights. Dive into this community with an open heart. Participate in collaborations, engage in challenges, and contribute to conversations. The connections you make will be a source of inspiration, support, and growth.

Overcoming obstacles: The creative journey is paved with challenges—from the frustration of hitting a plateau to the discouragement of perceived failure. These moments, though difficult, are crucial for growth. They force us to reconsider our approach, to learn resilience, and to find new sources of inspiration. Remember, every great artist has faced and overcome challenges. You are no different.

Crafting Your Path

The tools, techniques, and philosophies detailed in this book are but a starting point. The true art of one-line drawing lies in the endless possibilities it offers for personal expression and exploration. As you continue on this path, consider these final thoughts:

Innovation and experimentation: Let your curiosity lead the way. Experiment with different mediums, subjects, and styles. Innovation is born from the willingness to try something new and the courage to see it through, regardless of the outcome.

Reflection and adaptation: Take the time to reflect on your work. What themes do you find yourself drawn to? What techniques resonate with you? Use these insights to adapt and refine your approach, always aiming for a deeper connection with your work.

Sharing and inspiring: As you grow in your art, consider mentoring or sharing your knowledge with others. The act of teaching can be a powerful tool for self-discovery and can inspire the next generation of artists to explore their own paths in one-line art.

Final Words

In conclusion, the line that stretches from the tip of your pen to the surface beneath is more than just ink—it's a reflection of your journey, a testament to your growth, and a bridge to your future explorations in art. The world of one-line art is infinite, with each stroke offering a new perspective, a new challenge, and a new opportunity for discovery. Keep drawing, keep exploring, and above all, keep sharing the beauty of your journey with the world. The path of one-line art is yours to shape, and I can't wait to see where it leads you.

EXTRA ONE-LINE EXERCISES

As you've gone through the pages of this book, you've taken on a journey, discovering the beauty and complexity of one-line art. You've learned that this art form is more than just a technique; it's a way of seeing the world through a singular, unbroken line. To further enrich your learning and solidify the skills we've explored, I've compiled a set of 30 one-line art exercises designed to stretch your creativity, refine your technique, and deepen your understanding of this unique artistic expression.

The Purpose of These Exercises

These exercises serve multiple purposes. They're here to challenge you, to push you out of your comfort zone, and to encourage you to explore the vast possibilities within the simplicity of a single line. Whether you're drawing a serene nature scene, capturing the dynamic movement of a dancer, or sketching the intricate details of a city skyline, each exercise is crafted to help you apply the principles you've learned in new and exciting ways.

How to Use Them

Daily practice: Incorporate these exercises into your daily routine. Even spending a few minutes each day on one exercise can make a significant difference in your skill level and confidence.

Explore and experiment: Feel free to interpret each exercise in your own way. There's no right or wrong way to complete them. The goal is to experiment and find new ways to express your creativity.

Reflect and refine: After completing an exercise, take a moment to reflect on your work. What did you learn? What challenges did you face, and how did you overcome them? Use these reflections to refine your approach with each new exercise.

Share your journey: I encourage you to share your progress with the community. Post your exercises online, seek feedback, and connect with fellow artists. This shared experience can be incredibly rewarding and enlightening.

Remember, the ultimate goal of these exercises is not to achieve perfection, but growth. Each line you draw is a step forward on your artistic journey. Embrace the challenges, celebrate your progress, and most importantly, enjoy the process of creating.

I've chosen to put together 30 exercises because this can be a great monthly challenge to do by yourself or with fellow artists. Working together with a community of people who enjoy the same art style makes it that much easier to stay consistent in your path to becoming better at your craft.

I can't wait to see where these exercises take you. Let's continue to explore the infinite possibilities of one-line art together.

Morning rituals

Draw a series of objects you use every morning, such as a coffee cup, toothbrush, or your phone, with one continuous line.

Emotion faces

Create five faces, each expressing a different emotion, using only one line.

Nature walk

Depict a scene you might see on a walk in nature, such as a tree, a cloud, and a bird, all connected by a single line.

Hands in action

Draw a hand performing various tasks, like writing, holding
a cup, or playing an instrument, with one unbroken line.

Cityscape

Illustrate a simplified city skyline, including buildings
of different shapes and sizes, with a single line.

Reflections
Draw a simple object next to its reflection in water,
focusing on symmetry and distortion, using one line.

Animal parade

Create a lineup of animals, domestic or wild,
each connected to the next by a single line.

Fashion figures

Sketch a series of fashion figures in various poses, using one line to capture both the form and the clothing.

Dynamic poses

Draw figures in dynamic poses, such as dancing
or jumping, with a single continuous line.

Facial expressions
Practice drawing different facial expressions on a basic
head shape, using one line to change the mood each time.

Kitchen utensils

Illustrate a series of kitchen utensils, from
spoons to spatulas, connected by one line.

Musical instruments

Create one-line drawings of different musical instruments, capturing their unique shapes.

Bookshelf life

Depict a bookshelf and the various items it might hold, such as books, a plant, or a photo frame, with one line.

Café scene
Sketch a cozy café interior, including furniture and
patrons, using a single line to connect the elements.

Pet portraits
Draw portraits of pets, trying to capture their personality and features with one continuous line.

Letter forms

Experiment with creating each letter of the
alphabet in a one-line style, adding artistic flair.

Mythical creatures

Let your imagination run wild and draw mythical creatures, from dragons to unicorns, with one line.

Sporting action

Illustrate athletes in action, from a runner to a swimmer, using one line to convey movement.

Famous landmarks
Choose landmarks from around the world and
capture their essence with a single line.

Under the sea
Create an underwater scene, connecting sea creatures
and plants with one continuous line.

Space exploration
Draw elements related to space, such as planets,
stars, and spacecraft, with one line.

Faces in profile

Practice drawing faces from a side view, focusing
on the silhouette and features, with one line.

Floral bouquet

Compose a bouquet of different flowers, connecting them into a single, flowing line drawing.

Furniture design
Sketch a series of furniture pieces, from chairs to tables,
using one continuous line for each.

Shadow play

Draw objects along with their shadows, using
one line to link the object and its shadow.

Seasonal trees

Illustrate trees in four different seasons, showing changes in foliage and shape, with one line.

Birds on a wire
Depict a row of birds sitting on a telephone wire,
using one line to connect them.

Window views
Create scenes you might see looking out of different windows,
from cityscapes to countryside, with one line.

Abstract patterns

Use one line to create a series of abstract patterns,
experimenting with flow and repetition.

Personal objects

Choose objects that have a personal meaning to you and
draw them connected by a single line.

ABOUT THE AUTHOR

Attabeira German de Turowski is a one-line artist with a profound passion for this unique and mesmerizing art form. Over the years she has cultivated her expertise in one-line drawing which has led her to share this captivating style with a broad audience. Through more than eight online courses, she has taught over 10,000 students the intricacies of one-line art. She has also collaborated with renowned brands like Montblanc, Adobe, Skillshare, and Inkbox.

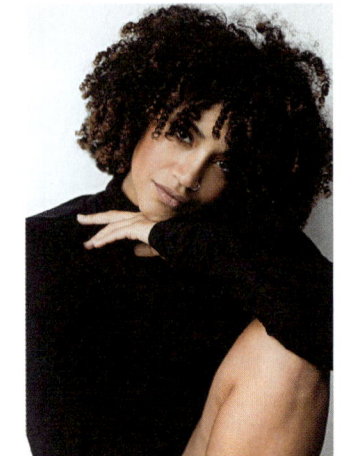

Connect with Attabeira and find more of her work online:

Website: attabeira.com

Instagram and TikTok: @attabeira_com

YouTube: @attabeiraoneline

ACKNOWLEDGMENTS

I'D LIKE TO express my profound gratitude to my husband Krzysztof Turowski for holding the fort while I go on my creative adventures. This book and pretty much my whole one-line art career would not exist without your unwavering support and encouragement. To Ama and Kai for being an infinite source of inspiration and my reason to do all this. And finally, but by no means less important, to my dad Eddie German for passing on to me my love for books. I hope this book makes you proud wherever your spirit may be. Your legacy lives on.